PURCHASING PRACTICES OF LARGE FOODSERVICE FIRMS

by

R. Dan Reid
Assistant Professor
The Whittemore School of Business & Economics
University of New Hampshire

and

Carl D. Riegel
Associate Professor of Management
College of Business Administration
Bowling Green State University

Copyright © 1989 by the National Association of Purchasing Management. All rights reserved. Contents may not be reproduced in whole or in part without the express permission of N.A.P.M.

ACKNOWLEDGMENTS •

THE CENTER FOR ADVANCED PURCHASING STUDIES and the authors wish to thank the purchasing executives in the 61 organizations who provided us the data on which this research report is based.

The work of Glenn Wilson in the coding of the data and the execution of the SAS programs was key to the timely completion of the overall study. Special thanks go to Joyce Hyslop and Ellen Engel for their assistance in the preparation of the manuscript. At CAPS, Carol Ketchum, Administrative Assistant; Mary Ann Beckley, Secretary; Richard Boyle, Research Assistant; and Laura Forker, Research Assistant.

Finally, seven purchasing executives/academics served on the ad-hoc industry/research advisory committee for this study. Their comments and review of the draft manuscript helped strengthen the analysis of the data. Special thanks are due to:

1. Lowell M. Hoffman, Kraft, Inc.
2. Julius J. Edelmann, Del Monte Foods
3. Lynal A. Root, McDonald's Corporation
4. Arthur Gibson, Proficient Food Company
5. Bruce Pauzus, Greyhound Food Management, Inc.
6. Michael G. Kolchin, Lehigh University
7. Ken Sovey, Taco Bell

Of course, complete responsibility for the final study results rests with the authors of this report.

ISBN: 0-945968-02-7
LCCN: 89-60232

CONTENTS •

Preface	7
Summary Findings	9
Implications And Suggestions Of The Survey Data	11
Design Of The Study	13
Method	13
Questionnaire	14
Response	14
Sample Characteristics	14
Purchasing Practices Of Large Foodservice Firms	15
The Purchasing Department	15
Purchase orders	16
Buyers	16
Chief purchasing officers	17
Summary and conclusion	17
Activities And Responsibilities Of The Corporate Foodservice Purchasing Department	17
Forecasting	18
Strategic decision-making	18
Purchasing of commodity groups	18
Key purchasing activities	19
Specifications	20
Summary	20
Supplier Relations And Selection	20
Number and type of vendors	21
Trends in vendor base	21
International vendors	21
Vendor visits	22
Sourcing issues	22
Sources by commodity	22
Supplier-selection	23
Assuring on-time and accurate delivery	23
Single sourcing	24
Summary	24
Ethics	24
Ethical issues	24
Perception of ethical/unethical behavior	25
Occurrence of ethical/unethical behavior	26
Code of ethics	26
Summary and conclusion	27
Future Research	27
Notes	28

EXHIBITS, TABLES, AND APPENDIX •

EXHIBIT 1:	Data Sought From Site Visits To Corporate Headquarters	13
EXHIBIT 2:	Characteristics Of Participating Firms	14
EXHIBIT 3:	Number Of Employees And Buyers In Foodservice Purchasing Departments	15
EXHIBIT 4:	Size Of Average Purchase Order	16
EXHIBIT 5:	Average Annual Number Of Purchase Orders	16
EXHIBIT 6:	Proportion Of Buyers' Time Spent Traveling	16
EXHIBIT 7:	Demographic Profile Of The Chief Purchasing Officer	17
EXHIBIT 8:	Involvement In Strategic Planning	18
EXHIBIT 9:	Responsibility Levels By Commodity	19
EXHIBIT 10:	Level Of Responsibility	19
EXHIBIT 11:	Use Of Specifications	20
EXHIBIT 12:	Number Of Vendors Used Annually	21
EXHIBIT 13:	Use Of New Vendors	21
EXHIBIT 14:	Increased/Decreased Use Of Vendors	21
EXHIBIT 15:	Use Of International Vendors	22
EXHIBIT 16:	Site Visitation To Vendors	22
EXHIBIT 17:	Commodity Sources	23
EXHIBIT 18:	Supplier-Selection Criteria	23
EXHIBIT 19:	Assuring On-Time Delivery	23
EXHIBIT 20:	Single Sourcing	24
EXHIBIT 21:	Ethical Dilemmas	25
EXHIBIT 22:	Perception Of Ethical Dilemmas	25
EXHIBIT 23:	Frequency Of Occurrence Ethical/Unethical	26
EXHIBIT 24:	Use Of Code Of Ethics	26
TABLE 1A:	Size Of Average Purchase Order By Category Of Organization	29
TABLE 1B:	Size Of Average Purchase Order By Annual Sales Of Organization	29
TABLE 1C:	Size Of Average Purchase Order By Number Of Units In Organization	30
TABLE 2A:	Average Annual Number Of Purchase Orders By Category Of Organization	30
TABLE 2B:	Average Annual Number Of Purchase Orders By Annual Sales Of Organization	31
TABLE 2C:	Average Annual Number Of Purchase Orders By Number Of Units In Organization	31
TABLE 3A:	Buyers' Travel By Category Of Organization	32
TABLE 3B:	Buyers' Travel By Annual Sales Of Organization	32

TABLE 3C:	Buyers' Travel By Number Of Units In Organization	32
TABLE 4A:	Distribution Of Forecasting Responsibility By Category Of Organization	32
TABLE 4B:	Distribution Of Forecasting Responsibility By Annual Sales Of Organization	33
TABLE 4C:	Distribution Of Forecasting Responsibility By Number Of Units In Organization	33
TABLE 5A:	Purchasing's Involvement In Strategic Planning By Category Of Organization	33
TABLE 5B:	Purchasing's Involvement In Strategic Planning By Annual Sales Of Organization	33
TABLE 5C:	Purchasing's Involvement In Strategic Planning By Number Of Units In Organization	34
TABLE 6A:	Organizational Level Responsible For Making Purchasing Decisions For Commodity Groups By Category Of Organization	35
TABLE 6B:	Organizational Level Responsible For Making Purchasing Decisions For Commodity Groups By Annual Sales Of Organization	36
TABLE 6C:	Organizational Level Responsible For Making Purchasing Decisions For Commodity Groups By Number Of Units In Organization	37
TABLE 7A:	Organizational Level Responsible For Key Purchasing Activities By Category Of Organization	38
TABLE 7B:	Organizational Level Responsible For Key Purchasing Activities By Annual Sales Of Organization	40
TABLE 7C:	Organizational Level Responsible For Key Purchasing Activities By Number Of Units In Organization	42
TABLE 8A:	Use Of Specifications By Category Of Organization	44
TABLE 8B:	Use Of Specifications By Annual Sales Of Organization	44
TABLE 8C:	Use Of Specifications By Number Of Units In Organization	44
TABLE 9A:	Total Number Of Vendors Used Annually By Category Of Organization	45
TABLE 9B:	Total Number Of Vendors Used Annually By Annual Sales Of Organization	45
TABLE 9C:	Total Number Of Vendors Used Annually By Number Of Units In Organization	45
TABLE 10A:	Use Of New Vendors By Category Of Organization	46
TABLE 10B:	Use Of New Vendors By Annual Sales Of Organization	46
TABLE 10C:	Use Of New Vendors By Number Of Units In Organization	46
TABLE 11A:	Total Number Of Vendors Used Annually By Category Of Organization	46
TABLE 11B:	Total Number Of Vendors Used Annually By Annual Sales Of Organization	47
TABLE 11C:	Total Number Of Vendors Used Annually By Number Of Units In Organization	47
TABLE 12A:	Use Of International Vendors By Category Of Organization	47
TABLE 12B:	Use Of International Vendors By Annual Sales Of Organization	47
TABLE 12C:	Use Of International Vendors By Number Of Units In Organization	48
TABLE 13A:	Site Visitation To Vendors By Category Of Organization	48

TABLE 13B:	Site Visitation To Vendors By Annual Sales Of Organization	48
TABLE 13C:	Site Visitation To Vendors By Number Of Units In Organization	48
TABLE 14A:	Use Of Single Source Suppliers By Category Of Organization	49
TABLE 14B:	Use Of Single Source Suppliers By Annual Sales Of Organization	49
TABLE 14C:	Use Of Single Source Suppliers By Number Of Units In Organization	49
TABLE 15A:	Source For Commodities By Category Of Organization	50
TABLE 15B:	Source For Commodities By Annual Sales Of Organization	51
TABLE 15C:	Source For Commodities By Number Of Units In Organization	52
TABLE 16A:	Supplier-Selection Criteria By Category Of Organization	53
TABLE 16B:	Supplier-Selection Criteria By Annual Sales Of Organization	53
TABLE 16C:	Supplier-Selection Criteria By Number Of Units In Organization	54
TABLE 17A:	Methods For Assuring On-Time Delivery By Category Of Organization	55
TABLE 17B:	Methods For Assuring On-Time Delivery By Annual Sales Of Organization	55
TABLE 17C:	Methods For Assuring On-Time Delivery By Number Of Units In Organization	55
TABLE 18A:	Mean Score Of Perceptions Of Ethical Dilemmas By Category Of Organization	56
TABLE 18B:	Mean Score Of Perceptions Of Ethical Dilemmas By Annual Sales Of Organization	56
TABLE 18C:	Mean Score Of Perceptions Of Ethical Dilemmas By Number Of Units In Organization	57
TABLE 19A:	Perceptions On Frequency Of Occurrence Of Industry Behaviors By Category Of Organization	57
TABLE 19B:	Perceptions On Frequency Of Occurrence Of Industry Behaviors By Annual Sales Of Organization	58
TABLE 19C:	Perceptions On Frequency Of Occurrence Of Industry Behaviors By Number Of Units In Organization	58
TABLE 20A:	Use Of Code Of Ethics By Category Of Organization	59
TABLE 20B:	Use Of Code Of Ethics By Annual Sales Of Organization	59
TABLE 20C:	Use Of Code Of Ethics By Number Of Units In Organization	59
TABLE 21A:	Gift Reporting Requirements By Category Of Organization	59
TABLE 21B:	Gift Reporting Requirements By Annual Sales Of Organization	60
TABLE 21C:	Gift Reporting Requirements By Number Of Units In Organization	60
APPENDIX:	Foodservice Purchasing Questionnaire	61
NOTES:		73
Center For Advanced Purchasing Studies		75

PREFACE

This report on *Purchasing Practices of Large Foodservice Firms* provides a better understanding of a broad-based industry, particularly within retail restaurants, foodservice in lodging, and institutional foodservice. It indicates that purchasing within the industry is viewed as a well-developed and specialized management function and that purchasers are primarily responsible for key materials management decisions. The fact that purchasing participates in high-level corporate decision-making explains, in part, the vitality of the foodservice industry.

However, the results should not be interpreted as an all-inclusive statement about foodservice purchasing. Instead, it is hoped that this report on foodservice purchasing practices encourages more research into the workings of the industry as well as provides a basis for comparing purchasing practices in foodservice with those in traditional manufacturing and service industries.

SUMMARY FINDINGS •

This report is based on data collected in the summer of 1988 from 61 multi-unit foodservice firms. These firms represented a variety of industry segments including retail restaurants, foodservice in lodging, and institutional foodservice. These firms averaged in excess of $100 million in annual sales and 43 percent of them reported average unit sales of more than $1 million per year. The significant findings of this study are:

1. *The average number of people employed in corporate purchasing offices was 22.* The number of employees ranged from one to 300 and up to a point the number of employees in purchasing increased with the size of the organization. Government-operated foodservice employed, on average, more personnel in the purchasing department, and privately operated institutional foodservice firms employed the least.

2. *The average number of buyers working in these purchasing departments was seven and responsibilities were assigned to buyers primarily on the basis of commodity groups.* In general, the number of buyers assigned to the department increased with the size of the organization. However, after a certain point, this number leveled out.

3. *The average dollar value for purchase orders issued by these companies was $3,000 and, on average, these firms issued between 2,000 and 4,000 purchase orders annually.* As the size of the firms increased, so did the dollar value and number of purchase orders. There appeared to be no relationship between the industry segment of the organization and the number or dollar value of purchase orders.

4. *Most chief purchasing officers in this sample held the title of either director or vice president of purchasing or distribution.* The majority of these CPOs were male, had completed college, were between 40 and 60 years old, and earned more than $50,000 per year. Lodging sector executives reported the highest annual salaries and were most likely to hold the title of vice president of food and beverage.

5. *Most responding organizations (85 percent) indicated that purchasing was involved, to one degree or another, in strategic planning.* Purchasing departments of firms operating primarily retail restaurants were more likely to be involved in strategic planning than their counterparts in either public sector foodservice or foodservice in lodging.

6. *More than half the participating companies reported that purchasing bore primary responsibility for forecasting product needs.* In lodging and in public sector organizations, however, the operations group was reported as bearing primary responsibility for making product forecasts. Finally, in larger firms, purchasing was more likely to bear primary responsibility for forecasting, both in terms of sales and in terms of units.

7. *In general, purchasing staffs were more involved with decisions regarding the purchase of high-cost commodities that could effectively be purchased in large lots or through national contracts.* Local management was more often involved with purchases of lower cost and the more perishable commodities. Hotel purchasing groups tended to be less involved in purchase decisions regarding all commodity groups. There was a direct relationship between the degree of purchase decision-making authority exercised and the size of the firm, as measured in the number of operating units.

8. *Corporate purchasing staffs held primary responsibility for traditional support activities such as supplier negotiation and evaluation, approving buying sources, and changing suppliers.* They were less likely to take on activities related to research and development, such as recipe or menu development, and less likely to be involved with control activities such as invoice approval or payment. Local management, by contrast, held little responsibility relating to purchasing except in areas dealing with order placement or control.

9. *Most firms in this sample employed formal, detailed, and written specifications.* Hotels were least likely to use formal specifications while public sector organizations were most likely to use them.

10. *About two-thirds of the companies responding currently use fewer than 300 vendors annually.*

11. *The size of the vendor base has grown moderately, while the composition has changed.* The

use of new vendors and the use of international vendors is growing.

12. *Approved national vendors are the primary source for most items while local vendors are used for produce and dairy products.* Larger companies tend to use corporate-owned commissaries/warehouses for many purchased items.

13. *Accurate on-time delivery, consistent quality with reasonable unit cost, and a willingness to work together are the most important supplier-selection criteria.* Tangential services are considered relatively unimportant.

14. *Developing a good vendor relationship and using purchasing clout are the two primary methods used for assuring on-time and accurate delivery.*

15. *Single sourcing is generally not used unless no other option exists or the item is proprietary in nature.*

16. *It is clear that most companies are in agreement as to what they perceive to be unethical behavior.* Divulging information on another supplier's quote, allowing the acceptance of physical gifts, overstating the seriousness of the situation to obtain concessions, and giving preference to suppliers favored by top management headed the list of unethical behavior. A number of activities were not clearly delineated as being either ethical or unethical. Government institutions had more definite ethical guidelines than did other categories of organizations.

17. *Respondents indicated that a number of practices that they considered unethical or questionable occurred with some frequency.* Government-sponsored organizations reported substantially fewer occurrences of unethical behavior, thus suggesting that clearer guidelines are beneficial.

18. *There was a high percentage of companies reporting that they actively applied a formal code of ethics to their purchasing departments.*

IMPLICATIONS AND SUGGESTIONS OF THE SURVEY DATA

This study was broad-based and primarily exploratory; however, its results suggest that purchasing is generally viewed as a well-developed and specialized management function in the foodservice industry and that decision-making in this area is correspondingly centralized. The study also indicates that corporate purchasing staffs bear primary responsibility for decisions concerning both key materials management activities and for decisions relating to purchases in key commodity groups. In contrast, middle-level and unit-line managers bear little purchasing responsibility other than for policy implementation or routine purchasing tasks.

With respect to supplier relations, the data suggest that the vendor base is growing gradually and the use of international vendors also is increasing. Furthermore, the primary source for most items is an approved national vendor and, therefore, developing good supplier relations is a matter of some importance.

Selection criteria deemed most important by this sample include on-time delivery, consistent quality, and reasonable unit cost.

With respect to ethics, the data suggest that most firms are in agreement as to what constitutes ethical or unethical behavior. However, it also appears that there is a perception that unethical behavior still occurs with some frequency in the foodservice industry.

Finally, the data suggest that there are substantial differences in the ways in which larger and smaller firms treat the purchasing function and that hotels, retail restaurants, and government-sponsored foodservice purchasing exhibit a number of differing characteristics.

DESIGN OF THE STUDY

A 1987 pilot study of 15 large foodservice organizations explored the key areas of foodservice purchasing from a corporate perspective and assessed the validity of future research in the area of purchasing in the hospitality industries.[1] The results of that study indicated that purchasing was viewed as a centralized staff activity at the corporate level and that decision-making appeared to be correspondingly centralized. Further, corporate purchasing staffs assumed the brunt of responsibility for decisions regarding both key materials management activities as well as purchasing in high-cost commodity groups. In contrast, middle-level and unit management in these organizations bore little or no responsibility for purchasing tasks.

The study concluded that a larger investigation of purchasing practices would add credence to its results and conclusions and that additional topics such as supplier relationships, contract compliance, purchasing department organization and ethics, to name a few, should be included.

As a result, this investigation was undertaken to shed more light on corporate purchasing practices in the foodservice industry by expanding the number of firms in the sample and to investigate areas that were not addressed in previous studies. Specifically, the purpose of this research was to obtain information regarding the following aspects of the purchasing function:

1. Descriptive characteristics of the purchasing department, including measures of size, criteria for assigning duties to buyers, and characteristics of the chief purchasing officer (CPO);

2. The activities and responsibilities of the corporate purchasing department, including the distribution of responsibilities between other functional areas and purchasing, and between the purchasing department and field operations;

3. Supplier relations and sourcing, including the number of vendors used, the use of single sources, sourcing by commodity group, supplier selection and methods used to ensure supplier performance; and

4. The perception of foodservice CPOs regarding what constitutes ethical or unethical behavior and the extent to which they believe unethical behavior occurs in foodservice purchasing.

Finally, this study was designed to ascertain whether or not key variables such as the type of organization (retail restaurants, foodservice in lodging, institutional foodservice, etc.), the annual sales of the responding organization, or the number of units in that organization revealed differences in purchasing department characteristics, activities and responsibilities, supplier relations, or ethical perceptions.

METHOD

The study was accomplished in two stages. First, a set of questions dealing with purchasing decision-making, buying procedures, supplier relations, and ethics was developed. (See Exhibit 1.) These questions, in turn, were validated by site visits to the corporate purchasing headquarters of several multi-site foodservice organizations. Based on data gathered from the site visits, specific questions were developed for a questionnaire that was mailed to the chief purchasing officer of the 400 foodservice and restaurant firms with the highest annual sales for 1987 as listed in the foodservice trade magazine *Restaurants and Institutions*.[2] These data were tabulated and analyzed and the results and conclusions appear in the body of this report.

EXHIBIT 1

DATA SOUGHT FROM SITE VISITS TO CORPORATE HEADQUARTERS

I. Purchasing Decision-Making
   A. Location of purchasing department within the firm
   B. How decisions relating to purchasing are shared with other corporate functional areas and with units in the field
   C. How employees are selected for the purchasing department
   D. How the purchasing department is organized
      1. number of employees
      2. key job titles
      3. how tasks and responsibilities are distributed
   E. The relationship of the purchasing department to line corporate functions

EXHIBIT 1 *(continued)*

DATA SOUGHT FROM SITE VISITS TO CORPORATE HEADQUARTERS

II. Buying Procedures
    A. Quality control
    B. Use of specifications
    C. How demand is forecasted
    D. Methods used to ensure product consistency
    E. How operating units order materials
    F. How fresh product waste is handled
    G. Use of commissaries and/or warehouses

III. Supplier Relations
    A. Selection criteria
    B. Vendor evaluation
    C. Supplier development
    D. How long-term relationships are developed and maintained
    E. Trends toward increases and decreases in the total number of vendors used
    F. Whether or not contracts are used and, if so, what types of contracts are employed
    G. How contracts and other agreements are monitored
    H. How contracts and other agreements are negotiated
    I. The use of international suppliers

IV. How Distribution to Field Units is Handled

V. Ethics
    A. To what extent ethics are a concern of the purchasing department
    B. What practices in particular pose ethical dilemmas
    C. What policies are in place to address ethical concerns
    D. Is there a published code of ethics

QUESTIONNAIRE

The questionnaire (see Appendix) focuses on seven areas:

1. demographic characteristics describing the responding firm;

2. purchasing department functions;

3. distribution of purchasing activities and responsibilities within the responding organization;

4. supplier relations and selection;

5. perceptions of what constitutes ethical and unethical behavior;

6. perceptions of the frequency of occurrence of ethical and unethical behavior; and

7. personal characteristics of the chief purchasing officer.

In general, most questions employed a five-point Likert-type scale.

RESPONSE

The questionnaires were mailed to the person named as being responsible for purchasing in the *Restaurants and Institutions "400" Executive Directory.*[3] Despite the care taken to ensure that questionnaires were sent to firms in which the chief purchasing director could be identified by name, 40, or 10 percent, were returned without forwarding information. Of the 360 questionnaires that reached organizations, 61 usable surveys were returned, making the response rate 18 percent.

SAMPLE CHARACTERISTICS

While completed questionnaires were received from a diverse cross section of the industry (see Exhibit 2), companies operating retail restaurants accounted for the bulk of responses, and the typical responding firm was primarily an operator of its own company-owned outlets.

EXHIBIT 2

CHARACTERISTICS OF PARTICIPATING FIRMS

	%	#
Industry Segment		
Institutional foodservice (private)	18	11
Institutional foodservice (government)	18	11
Retail restaurants	51	31
Foodservice in lodging	13	8
Type of Operator		
Primarily as a franchisor	10	6
Primarily company-owned units	73	45
Not applicable	17	10
Annual Foodservice Sales*		
Less than $100 million	50	29
Between $100 million and $1 billion	31	29
Greater than $1 billion	19	11
Number of Operating Units		
Less than 100 units	40	24
Between 100 and 249 units	24	15
Between 250 and 1,000 units	17	10
More than 1,000 units	19	12
Average Sales of Operating Units		
Less than $500,000	27	17
Between $500,000 and $999,999	30	18
Between $1 million and $1.49 million	18	11
Greater than $1.49 million	25	15

*Since many of the responding firms operate multiple lines of business, respondents were asked to report only foodservice sales.

Furthermore, about half the firms had sales in excess of $100 million and 60 percent operated more than 100 field units. Finally, 73 percent of the responding firms reported average unit sales in excess of $500,000 per year, and 43 percent indicated that average unit sales surpassed $1 million per year.

PURCHASING PRACTICES OF LARGE FOODSERVICE FIRMS

The foodservice industry is a major contributor to our post-industrial economy and provides a particularly fertile medium for studying purchasing practices in large-scale service organizations. This is because of its size and also because a major proportion of foodservice sales are concentrated in large corporations. These corporations typically operate numerous geographically dispersed production and sales units and often manage several different foodservice concepts or product lines. This combination of size, geographic dispersion, and organizational complexity poses some unique problems in the area of purchasing procedures and policy. For example, how is consistency in raw materials maintained by firms that operate in numerous geographic regions, and how is decision-making authority with regard to purchasing decisions shared between corporate offices and units in the field?

Effective purchasing has long been regarded as a critical element of success for foodservice firms. However, until recently, purchasing has been regarded primarily as a cost and quality control function. Now, with the ascendancy of chain organizations in the foodservice industry, purchasing is becoming more generally recognized as an integral part of corporate strategy because it affects not only profit margins but also asset turnover, and through this, return on investment.[4] Furthermore, the ability to effectively manipulate economies of scale and to isolate consistent and reliable sources of supply will ultimately have an impact on both a firm's competitive position and on its corporate image.

Despite their importance, data on purchasing practices and procedures in the foodservice industry are limited. Although there is an abundance of information relating to both product specifications and prescribed rules of practice, very little has been written about how foodservice organizations actively approach purchasing.[5] Furthermore, information on how foodservice firms actually treat purchasing as a corporate function is virtually nonexistent.

A major purpose of this study is to make an initial contribution toward correcting this deficit by shedding light on actual purchasing practices and policies in the foodservice industry. To accomplish that purpose, this report begins with a description of the purchasing department, including measures of size, criteria for assigning duties to buyers, and characteristics of the chief purchasing officer (CPO). The next section covers the responsibilities and activities assigned to the corporate purchasing office. Following this, supplier relations and supplier-selection criteria are discussed, and a discussion of ethics in foodservice purchasing is presented.

THE PURCHASING DEPARTMENT

Although this study will construct a statistical portrait of the average purchasing department, there was a wide degree of variability among the responding firms. In regard to staffing, for example, the number of people employed in the purchasing department ranged from a low of one employed to a high of 300, and the number of buyers ranged from one to 123. Interestingly, the notion of a correlation between company size and the number of employees is only partially borne out. As Exhibit 3 indicates, organizations with lower annual sales employ, on the average, slightly more employees (15 versus 13) than do firms with moderate sales. However, the number of buyers employed in the purchasing department increases with sales until the company reaches the $1-billion mark, and then the number appears to level off and remain constant.

EXHIBIT 3

NUMBER OF EMPLOYEES AND BUYERS IN FOODSERVICE PURCHASING DEPARTMENTS

Number of Employees in Purchasing Department		22	
Number of Buyers		7	

	Private Institution	Government Institution	Retail Restaurant	Foodservice In Lodging
Number of Employees in Purchasing Department	9	43	20	24
Number of Buyers	4	10	8	6

	Less than $100 Million	Between $100 Million and $1 Billion	More than $1 Billion
Number of Employees in Purchasing Department	15	13	52
Number of Buyers	4	11	11

Purchase Orders

Another descriptor of the size of purchasing departments can be derived from the number of purchase orders issued annually and from their average dollar value. As would be expected, given the nature of the sample, the average dollar value of purchase orders tended to be high, and the total number of purchase orders issued on an annual basis by firms in this sample also centered on the high end of the scale. The median dollar value of individual purchase orders was around $3,000, and 62 percent of the companies reported average purchase orders in excess of $2,000. Similarly, the average firm in this sample issued between 2,000 and 7,000 purchase orders annually, and 33 percent of the firms issued more than 8,000 purchase orders on an annual basis. (See Exhibits 4 and 5.)

EXHIBIT 4
SIZE OF AVERAGE PURCHASE ORDER

	%
Less than $ 250	3.8
$ 250 — 500	9.4
501 — 1,000	9.4
1,001 — 2,000	15.1
2,001 — 4,000	22.6
4,001 — 8,000	13.2
More than $8,000	26.4

EXHIBIT 5
AVERAGE ANNUAL NUMBER OF PURCHASE ORDERS

	%
Less than 100	10.5
100 — 250	3.5
251 — 500	3.5
501 — 1,000	10.5
1,001 — 2,000	14.0
2,001 — 4,000	14.0
4,001 — 8,000	10.5
More than 8,000	33.3

In general, the hypothesis that company size should correlate with the dollar value of purchase orders issued (see Tables 1a-1c) was affirmed. For example, in firms with less than $100 million in annual sales, purchase orders averaged less than $2,000. In firms with $100 million to $1 billion in sales, 76 percent of all purchase orders exceeded $2,000, and in firms with over $1 billion in sales, 50 percent of all purchase orders exceeded $8,000. Furthermore, in firms with less than 100 units, only 9 percent reported an average purchase order that exceeded $8,000, but in companies with 1,000 or more units, 71 percent reported average purchase orders of more than $8,000. Additionally, organizations operating primarily retail restaurants reported substantially higher purchase order values than did other categories. This adds credence to the notion that the purchasing function is highly centralized for this type of foodservice operation.

Similarly, the number of purchase orders issued annually was substantially higher for $1-billion-plus organizations than for the others. (See Tables 2a-2c.) However, no obvious relationship was suggested between the number of purchase orders issued and the type of organization or number of field units.

Buyers

Since buyers are key employees in purchasing departments, data were analyzed to ascertain how their responsibilities are assigned. For the most part, duties were assigned to buyers on the basis of commodity groups (54 percent). Only 4 percent of the sample indicated that buyers were assigned duties based on location, and the rest indicated other bases of assignment including such diverse mechanisms as division of the company, random assignment, or proportional division of full-line responsibilities.

Also, as a result of the geographic dispersion of the surveyed firms, it was assumed that many buyers would spend a substantial amount of time traveling either to deal with vendors in other locations or to visit field units. While there is some evidence to support this assumption, there is also a large proportion of buyers who spend little time traveling. Of the total sample, 46 percent of the responding firms reported that buyers spend 10 percent or more of their time traveling while the remainder indicated that buyers were on the road less than 10 percent of the time. (See Exhibit 6.)

The data suggest that buyers employed by retail restaurants and lodging operations are away more than either private or government-sponsored institutional buyers, and that the larger the firm, the more likely buyers are to spend time traveling. (See Tables 3a-3c.) This bolsters the notion that geographic dispersion is a key factor in determining buyers' travel since institutional operations would logically be less dispersed than restaurants and hotels and since larger companies would tend to comprise more dispersed outlets as well.

EXHIBIT 6
PROPORTION OF BUYERS' TIME SPENT TRAVELING

% Time Traveling	% of Buyers
Less than 10	54.2
10 - 30	30.5
31 - 50	11.9
51 - 70	1.7
More than 70	1.7

Chief Purchasing Officers

The typical purchasing department was headed by a director or vice president of purchasing or distribution. The majority of these CPOs were male, earned more than $50,000 per year, had worked in the purchasing field an average of 15 years, and were between 40 and 60 years old. Exhibit 7 details the characteristics of these purchasing officers.

By comparing characteristics by the type of organization, it appears that female purchasing executives were most widely accepted in government-operated institutional foodservice. Also, although the vast majority of CPOs were college-educated, the highest levels of educational attainment belonged to respondents from privately run institutional foodservice firms; respondents from foodservice in lodging had the lowest educational attainment. Also, the lodging sector reported the highest average salaries for CPOs, with 75 percent of them earning in excess of $60,000 per year, while public sector operations reported no salaries in excess of $60,000. Finally, the title of vice president of purchasing was most likely to be found in the retail restaurant group, while the title vice president of food and beverage was predominant in the lodging group. This reflects, possibly, the fact that food purchasing is a major corporate function for retail restaurants, while food purchasing is placed at a lower organizational level in lodging firms.

Summary And Conclusion

The descriptive data suggest that purchasing is a centralized activity for the foodservice firms in this study, as both the number of employees and the number of buyers in the department tend to increase with the size of the organization. Furthermore, buying activity is based more on commodity groups than on any other single factor, and this also adds credence to the hypothesis that purchasing is a centralized activity. Finally, the relationship between the size and number of purchase orders and the size of the organization suggests that the firms in this sample perform a large amount of buying services for units in the field.

The data relating to chief purchasing officers suggest that this position is viewed as an important one, held primarily by individuals with high-level academic and experiential credentials. However, it also appears that within lodging firms the purchasing function is primarily relegated to operating officers such as the vice presidents for food and beverage.

EXHIBIT 7
DEMOGRAPHIC PROFILE OF THE CHIEF PURCHASING OFFICER

	Private	Government	Retail	Lodging	Overall
Sex					
Male	90.91%	70.00%	93.55%	100.00%	88.50%
Female	9.09	30.00	6.45	0.00	11.50
Age					
20 - 32	9.09%	0.00%	20.00%	0.00%	11.70%
33 - 39	27.27	20.00	16.67	25.00	20.00
40 - 46	27.27	20.00	36.67	37.50	31.70
47 - 53	0.00	40.00	13.33	25.00	16.70
54 - 60	36.36	10.00	6.67	0.00	13.30
Greater than 60	0.00	10.00	6.67	12.50	6.70
Education					
H.S. diploma	0.00%	10.00%	10.00%	12.50%	8.30%
Some college	0.00	0.00	16.67	37.50	13.40
Bachelor's	54.55	40.00	36.67	50.00	41.70
Some grad.	18.18	50.00	23.33	0.00	23.30
Grad. degree	27.27	0.00	13.33	0.00	13.40
Job Title					
VP Purchasing	18.00%	0.00%	35.00%	14.00%	24.00%
Dir. Purchasing	36.00	11.00	35.00	14.00	29.00
Purchasing Mgr.	0.00	11.00	10.00	0.00	7.00
VP Food & Bev.	0.00	0.00	0.00	57.00	7.00
Dir. Foodservice	9.00	22.00	10.00	0.00	10.00
Other	37.00	56.00	10.00	15.00	23.00
Average # of Years with Firm					
Minimum	1.00%	5.00%	1.00%	1.00%	0.00%
Maximum	22.00	28.00	35.00	21.00	0.00
Average	10.28	17.67	10.82	9.75	11.68
Average # of Years in Purchasing					
Minimum	5.00%	2.00%	2.00%	8.00%	0.00%
Maximum	31.00	36.00	32.00	40.00	0.00
Average	15.78	21.22	11.73	17.00	14.77
Annual Salary					
Less than $30,000	0.00%	10.00%	3.23%	0.00%	3.30%
$30,000 - 39,999	20.00	30.00	9.68	12.50	15.00
40,000 - 49,999	30.00	40.00	22.58	12.50	25.00
50,000 - 59,999	10.00	20.00	22.58	0.00	18.30
60,000 - 69,999	20.00	0.00	9.68	25.00	11.70
70,000 - 85,000	20.00	0.00	6.45	25.00	10.00
More than $85,000	0.00	0.00	25.81	25.00	16.70

ACTIVITIES AND RESPONSIBILITIES OF THE CORPORATE FOODSERVICE PURCHASING DEPARTMENT

As is often the case, operations are the driving force in the foodservice industry and are, therefore, the predominant concern for foodservice companies. While purchasing seems to be a highly centralized function, operations are often not. They may be coordinated at a central level, but most day-to-day decisions are made at regional, district, and local levels.

Thus, the role of a central purchasing department is not clear and, in fact, may vary from firm to firm. In some organizations purchasing's role may be mostly advisory, and it may act more like a buying service than a fully integrated management function. On the other hand, in some companies purchasing may occupy a critical and authoritative position and may participate in decision-making that has organization-wide implications. In order to investigate the activities and responsibilities in this study, respondents were asked to indicate who in the organization had responsibility for forecasting, key purchasing activities, and purchasing decisions involving different commodities. Respondents were also questioned about whether or not purchasing participated in strategic planning and about the nature and use of product specifications in their firms. The following sections detail the results of this portion of the study.

Forecasting

Forecasting product needs is a good example of the need for shared information and shared responsibility between purchasing and other functional management areas and between purchasing and operations. Respondents were asked to indicate who in their company—marketing, operations, purchasing or another source—had primary responsibility for forecasting product needs. Overall, more than half (53 percent) of the responding firms said that purchasing had primary forecasting responsibility. Operations, on the other hand, had this duty in 37 percent of the companies and marketing in 5 percent. However, when the respondents are categorized by size or type of operation, a different picture emerges. More than half of the lodging and private organizations and 70 percent of the public sector organizations reported that operations held primary responsibility for forecasting. However, the larger the company (both in terms of annual sales and in terms of the number of operating units) the greater purchasing's involvement in forecasting. In firms exceeding 250 operating units, almost three-fourths indicated that purchasing made forecasts. Purchasing provided forecasts of product needs in more than 60 percent of the companies with sales of more than $1 billion. (See Tables 4a-4c.)

Strategic Decision-Making

If purchasing is generally recognized as an important element of strategic planning, then the purchasing department should be involved in strategic planning and strategic decision-making. The survey data suggest that this is, indeed, the case because 85 percent of the responding firms indicated that purchasing was involved, at some level, with strategic planning. (See Exhibit 8.) Purchasing groups in retail restaurants were more likely than their counterparts in lodging operations to be completely involved in strategic planning and, as might be expected, purchasers in government-run organizations were the least likely to be involved in strategy decisions. Interestingly, the annual sales of an organization did not appear to affect whether the purchasing department was involved in strategic planning or not. Of the firms reporting less than $100 million in sales, 82 percent indicated that purchasing was involved in strategic planning, and 82 percent of the $1-billion firms indicated that they also were involved. The data did, however, indicate a relationship between the number of units operated by a company and the degree to which the purchasing department was involved with strategic planning. Fully 100 percent of the firms with 250 or more operating units indicated that this was the case, while 20 percent of the smaller organizations said purchasing did not participate in strategic planning. (See Tables 5a-5c.)

EXHIBIT 8
INVOLVEMENT IN STRATEGIC PLANNING

	%
Completely involved	39.0
Somewhat involved	45.8
Not involved	15.2

Purchasing Of Commodity Groups

In general, corporate purchasing staffs were involved with commodity purchase decisions involving high-cost items or items that could effectively be purchased through the use of national or regional vendors. For example, 67 percent of the study participants indicated that the purchasing staff had primary purchasing responsibility for meat and poultry while only 37 percent reported such responsibility for produce items. Similarly, 73 percent of the corporate purchasing groups were involved in purchase decisions relating to major equipment while only 48 percent were involved with decisions concerning dairy products. (See Exhibit 9.)

EXHIBIT 9

RESPONSIBILITY LEVELS BY COMMODITY

	Corporate Purchasing Office	Corporate Line Officer	Regional Staff Mgmt.	Local Mgmt.	Other
Meat & Poultry	66.7%	10.0%	3.3%	15.0%	5.0%
Produce	36.7	5.0	8.3	41.7	8.3
Dairy Products	47.5	3.3	6.6	32.8	9.8
Groceries	65.0	1.7	8.3	16.7	8.3
Major Equipment	73.8	9.8	8.2	3.3	4.9
Small Wares	62.3	4.9	8.2	19.7	4.9
Nonconsumable Supplies	63.9	4.9	3.3	24.6	3.3

In contrast, hotel respondents reported much less involvement by corporate purchasing staffs in all commodity areas. This reflects the possibility that hotels tend to be larger operating entities than restaurants and that the need for similarity in foodservice is less for hotels than for retail restaurants. This contention is borne out by the fact that retail restaurants exhibit the highest degree of involvement by corporate purchasing departments in all commodity purchases. (See Table 6a.) Unlike lodging operations, retail restaurants have a high need for consistency and uniformity in finished product.

There also appears to be a direct relationship between size, as measured by the number of operating units, and the degree of responsibility that purchasing has for decisions involving all commodity groups. Purchasing is less involved with product purchase decisions in smaller firms and more involved in these decisions in larger firms. (See Table 6c.) For example, purchasing makes 100 percent of product decisions regarding meat in firms with more than 1,000 units and only 56 percent of such decisions in firms with less than 100 units.

Interestingly, this relationship is not sustained when respondents are categorized by annual sales. (See Table 6b.) Respondents with sales between $100 million and $1 billion exert far more influence on product purchases than do the $1-billion-plus firms or companies with sales of less than $100 million. This may be due to the possibility that a large number of hotel firms are members of the $1-billion-plus category or that many such firms operate multiple product lines.

Key Purchasing Activities

With respect to purchasing activities, corporate purchasing staffs were most likely to hold primary responsibility for traditional support areas such as negotiating with suppliers, approving buying sources, changing suppliers, and evaluating suppliers. They were less likely to be involved in research and development areas such as recipe or menu development, and in control areas such as invoice approval and payment. In contrast, unit managers held little purchasing responsibility except in areas dealing with control or order placing as shown in Exhibit 10.

EXHIBIT 10

LEVEL OF RESPONSIBILITY

	Corporate Purchasing Office	Corporate Line Officer	Regional Staff Mgmt.	Local Mgmt.	Other
Recipe development	25.0%	31.7%	11.7%	16.7%	15.0%
Menu development	21.7	38.3	11.7	15.0	13.3
Specification writing	48.3	23.3	8.3	10.0	10.0
Approval of buying source	71.7	10.0	1.7	8.3	8.3
Designation of approved brands	46.7	21.7	10.0	8.3	13.3
Supplier evaluation	66.7	8.3	3.3	18.3	3.3
Negotiation with suppliers	76.3	3.4	8.5	10.2	1.7
Change of suppliers	72.9	6.8	6.8	11.9	1.7
Change of brands	56.7	15.0	11.7	8.3	8.3
Substitution of approved items	50.0	11.7	18.3	11.7	8.3
Approve new products	41.7	25.0	10.0	11.7	11.7
Invoice approval	25.0	10.0	11.7	51.7	1.7
Invoice payment	36.7	13.3	10.0	25.0	15.0
Order placement with supplier	37.3	3.4	3.4	52.5	3.4

When the responses are scrutinized by categories, several patterns of difference emerge. (See Table 7a.) First, foodservice in lodging responses suggest that lodging operations are less prone to give corporate purchasing primary responsibility for key purchasing activities, and retail restaurants are more prone to give such responsibility to corporate staffs. Again, this is most likely due to the fact that food purchasing is a major corporate function for retail restaurants while, at least in this sample, food purchasing is subsumed at lower levels of the organization in lodging firms.

Also, when responses are compared by sales volume, corporate purchasing staffs of medium-sized firms hold more responsibility for traditional purchasing activities than do either small firms or large firms.

In the case of smaller firms, this appears to be a result of corporate line officers retaining this responsibility; in the case of larger firms, the data suggest that in many instances a portion of these responsibilities is delegated to regional staffs. (See Tables 7b-7c.)

Specifications

As a rule, most firms (63 percent) in this sample used formal and detailed written specifications for purchased products. Only about 7 percent had unwritten specifications and the remainder deviated either in formality or in flexibility. (See Exhibit 11.) However, when the data are viewed by category, a great deal of variability arises. (See Table 8a.) Lodging firms were least likely to use formal and detailed written specifications (25 percent), while government institutions and retail restaurants were most likely to use formal and detailed specifications (80 percent and 76 percent respectively). Also, the higher the sales volume and the higher the number of units, the more formal and detailed the specifications. In fact, all of the firms using unwritten specifications had 100 units or fewer. (See Tables 8a-8c.)

EXHIBIT 11

USE OF SPECIFICATIONS

	%
Formal, detailed, written specifications	62.7
Informal, flexible, unwritten specifications	6.8
Formal, flexible, written specifications	18.6
Somewhere in between formal and informal	11.9
None are used	0.0

Summary

In aggregate, the data suggest that corporate purchasing staffs are very much involved in corporate planning and decision-making as it relates to product purchasing and control. This suggests that, overall, there is a recognition that purchasing decisions have organization-wide implications, purchasing is viewed as more than a support area, and purchasing departments assume more than an advisory role in company-wide activities. Also, the distribution of responsibility in regard to purchasing particular commodity groups and in regard to key purchasing activities indicates that purchasing responsibilities are, for the most part, shared with other organizational entities where it makes sense. For example, purchasing has responsibility for commodity groups that are costly and that lend themselves either to mass purchases or contract purchases. Purchasing does not assume final responsibility for less costly or perishable items that are best purchased on local markets.

Two factors appear to exert the greatest influence on the degree of authority and responsibility exercised by the purchasing staff: 1) the size of the organization and 2) the type of business in which the organization is primarily involved.

The size of the organization influences the degree to which central purchasing officers are involved in organization-wide activities such as forecasting or strategic planning, the degree to which a central purchasing office has control over traditional purchasing support functions, and the formality with which purchasing is approached. This conclusion makes sense in light of the fact that larger organizations have more need for centralization and control in this area and because large organizations also have the slack to provide for specialized expertise in this area.

The type of business influences purchasing practices in at least two ways. First, public sector food-service organizations seem to involve purchasing less in organization-wide decisions, and purchasing in public sector organizations appears to be more highly controlled and more formal. Thus, while these government-sponsored foodservice purchasing groups may not be involved in strategic planning, they exert a great deal of influence in most commodity group purchases and tend to have formal and detailed specifications. Second, as in the public sector organizations, hotel foodservice purchasing staffs are less likely than others to participate in organizational decision-making and less likely to have final responsibility for key purchases or key activities. However, in contrast to public sector organizations, hotels also tend to have less formal purchasing requirements and tend to place more responsibility on other line management and on local management.

SUPPLIER RELATIONS AND SELECTION

Once a decision of relatively insignificant consequence, the supplier-selection decision has, in recent years, become increasingly important. Since suppliers have adopted vastly different delivery and billing practices, and since the quality of food items tends to vary, selecting the right supplier can have significant impact on bottom-line performance. The pilot study suggests that buyers prefer suppliers who provide accurate on-time delivery. These criteria suggest that good vendor relationships are becoming a necessity. This study examines several aspects of vendor relationships, such as the total number of vendors used annually, the number of new vendors used, the pattern of growth relative to the size of the vendor base, the use of international vendors, and the percentage of vendor facilities visited annually. Each of these activities is expected to have an impact on vendor relationships.

Number And Type Of Vendors

A primary consideration in the development of good vendor relationships is the total number of vendors that are used by a company. The greater the number of vendors, the less likely it is that good relationships can be formed with all of the vendors. About 40 percent of the companies in this study deal with 100 or fewer vendors annually, and 20 percent of the companies deal with more than 500 vendors annually. The bulk of responses indicated that two-thirds of the companies work with 300 or fewer vendors annually. Detailed data by category of organization, annual sales, and number of units can be found in Tables 9a, 9b, and 9c, respectively. The data in Table 9a indicated that the category of organization is not a significant factor in the number of vendors used. However, the total number of vendors used increases as annual sales increase. (See Table 9b.)

Approximately 64 percent of the companies with sales in excess of $1 billion used more than 300 vendors per year, while only about 24 percent of companies with sales under $100 million used more than 300 vendors annually. The larger companies may be forced to use more vendors by virtue of the diversity of their product line. The effect of the number of units in the organization remains relatively constant once a firm has more than 100 operating units. (See Table 9c.)

EXHIBIT 12
NUMBER OF VENDORS USED ANNUALLY

	%
Fewer than 50	18.3
Between 50 and 100	21.7
Between 101 and 150	8.3
Between 151 and 200	6.7
Between 201 and 300	10.0
Between 301 and 400	8.3
Between 401 and 500	6.7
Greater than 500	20.0

Trends In Vendor Base

The development of good vendor relationships is usually a long-term process so a large increase in the number of new vendors would not be expected if good vendor relationships have been established and maintained. Exhibit 13 reports the use patterns of new vendors by the companies responding to this study. Some 75 percent of the companies reported that new vendor use has increased at least moderately in the recent past. Given the total number of vendors used and the slight growth reported in the size of the vendor base (see Exhibit 14), it is possible that increased use of new vendors is a natural result of organizational growth and/or increased product diversity rather than a result of poor vendor relations. One exception to this is in government institutions, in which 90 percent of the operations reported increased use of new vendors. This increase may be due to increased emphasis on vendor evaluation at these institutions and the use of competitive bidding. Detailed data regarding the use of new vendors are available in Tables 10a, 10b, and 10c.

EXHIBIT 13
USE OF NEW VENDORS

	%
The use has increased significantly	14.8
The use has increased moderately	60.7
The use has remained constant	18.0
The use has decreased moderately	6.6
The use has decreased significantly	0.0

The size of the vendor base impacts the development of good supplier relations. The smaller the vendor base, the larger the amount of time that a company can spend on developing a good relationship. Exhibit 14 shows that almost 75 percent of the companies reported at least moderate increases in the number of vendors used, and the remaining companies reported at least a moderate decrease. The companies reporting increases may have increased the number of vendors in order to provide multiple sources of critical elements, or required additional vendors because of increased product diversity. Increases could also have resulted from the replacement of poorly performing suppliers. Decreases in the vendor base are often implemented to allow for better control of vendors and to afford a better opportunity for maintaining good vendor relationships. The detailed data regarding trends in the size of the vendor base are available in Tables 11a, 11b, and 11c.

EXHIBIT 14
INCREASED/DECREASED USE OF VENDORS

	%
The number has increased at a high rate	13.1
The number has increased moderately	60.7
The number has decreased slightly	21.3
The number has decreased significantly	4.7

International Vendors

Another concern with regard to the vendor base was the use of international vendors. Exhibit 15 reports the use of international vendors by the respondents. While some 48 percent of the companies have decreased their use of offshore vendors, approximately 44 percent have increased their use of international vendors. The detailed data in Table 12a suggest that retail restaurants and foodservice in lodging operations are increasing their use of international vendors. This is possibly due to increased demand for product offerings that are not available or are in short supply within the United States. Data in Table 12b suggest that companies with higher annual sales are increasing their use of international suppliers. This probably results because these companies have the necessary resources to maintain current knowledge of world markets and have larger consumption requirements that make such purchases economically feasible. Data in Table 12c offer further support of the use of international vendors by large companies.

EXHIBIT 15

USE OF INTERNATIONAL VENDORS

	%
The use has increased significantly	5.1
The use has increased moderately	39.0
The number has remained constant	8.5
The use has decreased moderately	3.4
The use has decreased significantly	44.0

Vendor Visits

Visits by purchasing department staff to suppliers provide, to a large extent, visible support of buyers' commitment to establishing mutually satisfactory relationships with vendors. It was assumed that a reasonable percentage of the vendors would be visited annually in order to sustain the working relationship. However, about 56 percent of the companies visited less than 10 percent of their vendors during the year and only 11.5 percent visited 75 percent or more of their vendors. (See Exhibit 16.) Tables 13a, 13b, and 13c provide some insight into this behavior. Smaller companies may not have adequate resources to physically visit each of their vendors throughout the year. They may only visit those vendors who have provided poor service or quality. The high percentage of companies visiting less than 10 percent of their vendors support this conclusion. On the other hand, larger companies have more resources to visit vendors and often can economically justify the visit due to the volume of purchases made with a particular vendor. Given the relatively stable size of the vendor base, regardless of category of organization, and the larger purchases required by larger firms, vendor visits are more easily cost-justified.

EXHIBIT 16

SITE VISITATION TO VENDORS

	%
Less than 10 percent	55.7
Between 10 and 25 percent	14.8
Between 26 and 50 percent	9.8
Between 51 and 75 percent	8.2
More than 75 percent	11.5

Sourcing Issues

Before supplier relationships can be established, foodservice firms must first identify sources of supply and develop criteria for selecting suppliers for vendor commodity groups. The unique operating characteristics of large-scale foodservice firms pose some equally unique purchasing requirements. First, adequate sources must be identified for a variety of commodity groups, ranging from highly perishable daily-use items to major equipment. Second, selection criteria must be developed for selecting suppliers who can meet the demands of an industry characterized by multiple-operating and, hence, multiple-delivery units. Finally, once selection criteria have been identified, methods of assuring that vendors adhere to the criteria that related to their selection in the first place must be employed.

The following section reports on the sources for purchasing particular commodity groups, supplier-selection criteria, and methods used to ensure supplier performance.

Sources By Commodity

Companies were asked to identify their primary source for the commodity groups shown in Exhibit 17. Generally, approved local vendors were the primary sources for produce and dairy products, while approved national vendors were the primary sources of meat and poultry, groceries, major equipment, small wares, and nonconsumable supplies. Detailed data by category of organization, annual sales, and number of units in the organization are available in Tables 15a, 15b, and 15c. These data indicate that government institutions are more likely to use approved local vendors for meat and poultry, and to use approved regional vendors more for dairy products. This seems reasonable given that most institutional foodservices operate in a limited geographical area and do not have the nationwide operating units to justify national suppliers. A similar situation is true for the private institutions, as they tend to use approved local vendors more for groceries. Like government-sponsored institutional operators, these firms are often limited to smaller geographical areas and have fewer operating units, thus facilitating the use of local vendors. Larger companies, both in terms of annual sales and number of operating units, tend to use corporate commissaries/warehouses more frequently for meat and poultry, and groceries—a reasonable result, given the companies' ability to employ economies of scale.

EXHIBIT 17
COMMODITY SOURCES

	Corporate-Owned Commissary or Warehouse	Approved National Vendor	Approved Regional Vendor	Approved Local Vendor	Other
Meat and Poultry	22.0%	33.9%	22.0%	20.3%	1.7%
Produce	6.9	3.4	20.7	65.5	3.4
Dairy Products	8.3	10.0	28.3	51.7	1.7
Groceries	16.9	40.7	20.3	18.6	3.4
Major Equipment	13.3	61.7	15.0	6.7	3.3
Small Wares	15.0	40.0	25.0	18.3	1.7
Nonconsumable Supplies	15.0	40.0	16.7	23.3	5.0

Supplier-Selection

Once the sources of different commodities have been identified, the actual selection of the vendor follows. In this study we asked our respondents to react to 20 supplier characteristics in terms of their importance in evaluating a supplier for selection. We then computed a rank-order score for each attribute by adding the percentage of respondents that rated that attribute as "extremely important," "moderately important," or "not important." Exhibit 18 depicts this ranking. Accurate and on-time delivery, consistent quality with reasonable prices, and a willingness to work together were the desired supplier characteristics. Selection of these characteristics supports the results reported in the pilot study. While the top six characteristics overall were considered important by all categories of organizations, it appears (see Table 16a) that private institutions listed additional attributes as more than moderately important. These include reasonable minimum orders, volume discounts, frequency of delivery, etc. Such attributes would be more important to companies with less operating capital to invest in inventories. Similarly, companies with greater than 1,000 operating units consider additional criteria as more than moderately important. These additional attributes deal with volume discounts, payment policies, technical competency, and geographical distance. (See Table 16c.) The least important attributes, overall, tended to be the tangential services provided by suppliers. Given the annual sales volume of the companies in this study, little need for these services existed.

EXHIBIT 18
SUPPLIER-SELECTION CRITERIA

Accuracy in filling orders	1.17
Consistent quality level	1.17
On-time delivery	1.23
Willingness to work together to resolve problems	1.36
Willingness to respond in a pinch	1.53
Reasonable unit cost	1.60
Reasonable lead times	2.00
Frequency of delivery	2.09
Technical competence	2.09
Lowest unit cost	2.15
Reasonable payment policy	2.28
Volume discounts	2.30
Knowledgeable sales staff	2.32
Reasonable minimum order	2.55
Geographical distance	2.69
Prompt payment discounts	2.70
Ability to single source	3.23
Training in product use	3.26
Willingness to break a case	3.66
Provision of recipe ideas	3.85

Assuring On-Time And Accurate Delivery

The pilot study reported the importance of on-time and accurate delivery performance by suppliers.[6] However, that study did not ascertain how such performance was achieved. This study suggested seven possible methods for achieving this performance as shown in Exhibit 19. The most frequently employed practice involved developing good vendor relationships, closely followed by exercising purchasing clout. These two common practices represent extremes in vendor treatment. The detailed data are available in Tables 17a, 17b, and 17c. Foodservice in lodging operations was most likely to use purchasing clout and to negotiate long-term contracts with performance clauses to assure delivery. Larger companies, by contrast, tended to use purchasing clout and good vendor relationships. This suggests two distinct schools of thought. Finally, very few companies were willing to pay a somewhat higher unit cost to assure delivery.

EXHIBIT 19
ASSURING ON-TIME DELIVERY

Developing a good vendor relationship (for example, prompt payment, reasonable requests, shared cost data, etc.)	1.32
Using your purchasing clout	1.62
Using multiple sources	2.17
Negotiating long-term contracts with performance clauses	2.59
Using exclusivity contracts	2.67
Paying a somewhat higher per unit price	3.70
Providing corporate incentives (for example, offering discounts at your facilities)	4.28

Single Sourcing

One view of developing beneficial supplier relationships suggests that it is easier to accomplish such interaction with a smaller vendor base. One way to decrease the number of vendors used is to single source items. The use of single sourcing by the respondents is shown in Exhibit 20. Most of the companies use single sourcing only when no other option exists or for proprietary items. The detailed data are available in Tables 14a, 14b, and 14c. As expected, government institutions do not single source unless no other option exists; the same is true for foodservice in lodging operations. While some companies have decreased their vendor base, it appears that most companies still do not follow a single-sourcing strategy but maintain multiple suppliers for most items.

EXHIBIT 20

SINGLE SOURCING

	%
Single sourcing is used only when no other option is available	41.7
Single sourcing is used only for standard items that can be easily bought elsewhere	6.7
Single sourcing is used for proprietary items	35.0
Other	16.7

Summary

Supplier relations and selection suggest that most of the companies are using 300 or fewer vendors annually. The vendor base has been growing moderately in the recent past, as has the use of new vendors. Large companies, in particular, are using more international vendors than previously. Foodservice companies, in general, do not visit many of their vendors during the year. This may be due to resource-allocation decisions or to these companies' concentration on visiting vendors who pose problems. If this is the case, the low percentage of vendors visited are a good sign. However, the need to visit vendors and better understand their processes and associated problems is likely to become increasingly important in the future if good vendor relationships are to be maintained.

Most of the companies use either approved national vendors or approved local vendors as their primary sources of supply. Suppliers tend to be selected based on their accurate on-time delivery, their willingness to work together, their reasonable cost, and their consistent quality. Few of the companies need the tangential services offered. The primary means for assuring accurate on-time delivery represent two different schools of thought. One method is through the development of a good vendor relationship, while the other is through the use of the company's purchasing clout. It appears that eventually the development of good vendor relationships will dominate. As vendor relationships continue to improve, so should the use of single sourcing. Current practices tend to avoid the use of single sourcing.

ETHICS

Ethical Issues

Many ethical dilemmas are faced daily by members of purchasing departments as suggested by a recent article in the *Chicago Tribune*. On June 13, 1988, the article "Schools Play Favorites With Food Contracts" alleged abuses in the purchasing practices of the Chicago Public School System, which purchases in excess of $42 million worth of food annually. The article said, "The Chicago public school system regularly bypasses low bidders in awarding millions of dollars' worth of food-supply contracts and uses a selection system that often increases costs by a third and drives off competitors."[7]

Ethical dilemmas faced by members of the purchasing department can be grouped into three general categories. The first category includes efforts to gain inside information about competitors that will benefit the firm's competitive position—for example, receiving information about competitors through shared suppliers. The second category includes activities that allow the purchasing officer to gain personal benefits from suppliers. These personal benefits can be free lunches, dinners, entertainment, trips, volume incentives, and gifts. The third category includes activities that manipulate the vendors in such a manner as to benefit the purchasing firm. Examples of such activities include overstating the seriousness of a problem to obtain concessions from the vendor, threatening the use of a second source, using the firm's economic clout, allowing information on bids from other suppliers, etc.

Questions with regard to ethical dilemmas were included in this study to measure practitioners' perceptions as to which activities represented ethical or unethical behavior and with regard to the frequency of occurrences of those activities within the industry. The 11 ethical dilemmas presented to the chief purchasing officers in this study are shown in Exhibit 21. These dilemmas were first used by Dubinsky and Gwin.[8]

EXHIBIT 21
ETHICAL DILEMMAS

1. Gaining information about competitors by asking suppliers for information.
2. Allowing physical gifts such as free sales promotion prizes or purchase-volume incentive bonuses to be accepted by a purchaser.
3. Making statements to an existing supplier that exaggerate the seriousness of a problem in order to obtain better prices or other concessions.
4. Giving preferential treatment to suppliers that higher levels of management within your firm prefer or recommend.
5. Giving preferential treatment to suppliers who are also good customers.
6. Allowing free trips, free lunches or dinners, or other free entertainment to be accepted by a purchaser.
7. Allowing personalities—liking for one sales representative and disliking for another—to enter into the supplier-selection process.
8. Allowing one or more suppliers to have information on competitors' quotations and allowing such suppliers to requote.
9. Showing bias against suppliers whose salespeople attempt to reach and influence other departments—such as new product development—directly rather than go through the purchasing department when such avoidance of the purchasing department increases the likelihood of a sale.
10. Telling an existing supplier the firm is considering using a second source in order to obtain better prices or other concessions.
11. Using the firm's economic buying power to obtain better prices or other concessions.

Perception Of Ethical/Unethical Behavior

The chief purchasing officers indicated their perceptions of the ethical nature of each of the 11 activities in Exhibit 21 by responding to a five-point Likert scale. Responses of "very unethical" (lowest value = 1) to "ethical" (highest value = 5) were used. The mean value for responses to each of the dilemmas is shown in Exhibit 22, and detailed data by category of organization, annual sales of organization, and number of units in the organization are shown in Tables 18a, 18b, and 18c. In general, the purchasing officers considered four activities to be unethical or very unethical. Allowing suppliers information concerning the quotes of other suppliers was considered to be the most unethical practice. It was followed closely by members of the purchasing department accepting physical gifts; companies overstating the seriousness of a problem in order to obtain concessions from a supplier; and preference being given to suppliers favored by top management. These results are generally similar to those found in a study of purchasing practitioners by Presutti.[9] However, in his study, the mean response to allowing suppliers information concerning the quotes of other suppliers was significantly higher (2.75), thus suggesting it to be perceived more ethical by purchasers in other industries than in our study where the mean response was 1.50. It should be noted that the respondents from government institutions considered eight of the activities to be at least somewhat unethical (see Table 18a), while purchasing officers in the retail restaurants and foodservice in lodging considered only three of the activities to be somewhat unethical.

When one examines the responses in terms of annual sales (see Table 18b), companies with sales in excess of $1 billion regarded six of the activities as unethical, while companies with sales ranging from $100 million to $1 billion only found three of the activities somewhat unethical. With regard to the number of units in the organization (see Table 18c), companies with 100 to 249 operating units considered six of the activities somewhat unethical.

The two activities generally considered ethical by the purchasing officers in this study correspond to those found in the Presutti study. Threatening the use of a second vendor in order to obtain concessions from the supplier and using the firm's economic clout were both considered ethical practices. While the ethical nature of the remaining activities was not clear, the mean response values below three indicated that these activities were at least viewed as somewhat unethical by many of the respondents.

EXHIBIT 22
PERCEPTION OF ETHICAL DILEMMAS

Allowing information on quotes	1.50
Allowing physical gifts	1.62
Overstating seriousness of problem	1.71
Preference to suppliers favored by top management	1.98
Allowing free trips, entertainment, etc.	2.31
Allowing personalities to enter into decision	2.44
Preference to suppliers who are good customers	2.60
Bias against companies shortcutting purchasing department	2.75
Gaining information about your competitor from your supplier	2.93
Threatening to use second source	3.80
Using firm's economic clout	4.83

Key:

1 = Very unethical
5 = Ethical

Occurrence Of Ethical/Unethical Behavior

The chief purchasing officers also indicated their perceptions concerning the frequency of occurrence for each of the 11 activities listed in Exhibit 21. Again, a five-point Likert scale was used and a response of 1 indicated that the practice was very widespread, while a response of 5 indicated that the practice was rarely observed.

The purchasing officers perceived that two of the four activities identified as most unethical—"allowing physical gifts" and "overstating the seriousness of the problem"—occurred with average frequency. The other two activities—"allowing information on quotes" and "giving preference to suppliers favored by top management"—occurred just slightly less than average. Detailed data with regard to category of organization, annual sales, and number of units in the organization are shown in Tables 19a, 19b, and 19c, respectively. Of note is the somewhat limited reporting of occurrences of many of the unethical activities with regard to government institutions. This suggests that an actively applied code of ethics may be effective in decreasing the frequency of occurrence of unethical behaviors.

The occurrence of the two ethical activities identified by the respondents—"using firm's economic clout" and "threatening to use a second source"—was perceived as being widespread or very widespread. The mean values regarding the perceived frequency of occurrence of the ethical dilemmas are provided in Exhibit 23. The frequency of use for each of these activities by government institutions was significantly less than for all other categories of organizations.

EXHIBIT 23
FREQUENCY OF OCCURRENCE ETHICAL/UNETHICAL

Using firm's economic clout	1.36
Threatening to use second source	2.22
Gaining information about your competitor from your supplier	2.47
Overstating seriousness of problem	2.74
Allowing physical gifts	2.89
Allowing free trips, entertainment, etc.	2.89
Allowing personalities to enter into decision	2.95
Preference to suppliers favored by top management	3.13
Bias against companies shortcutting purchasing department	3.15
Preference to suppliers who are good customers	3.24
Allowing information on quotes	3.35

Key:
1 = Very widespread
5 = Rarely observed

Code Of Ethics

Given the frequency of ethical dilemmas faced by members of purchasing departments, it seems reasonable that companies operating in the foodservice industry would have a code of ethics to provide guidelines relative to expected behavior. Exhibit 24 provides the results of the study with regard to the percentage of companies that have a code of ethics and how actively it is applied. While it is encouraging that 61.7 percent of the companies responding have a written code of ethics that is actively applied, it is somewhat disturbing that 28.4 percent of the companies have only an unwritten code of ethics and that the remaining 10 percent of the companies have a code of ethics that is not actively applied.

EXHIBIT 24
USE OF CODE OF ETHICS

	%
Company has a code of ethics that is actively applied	61.7
Company has a code of ethics that is used occasionally	6.7
Company has a code of ethics but does not monitor it	3.3
Company has an unwritten code of ethics	28.4

Tables 20a, 20b, and 20c provide more detailed information on the use of the code of ethics by category of organization, annual sales of organization, and number of units in the organization. From these tables, it appears that companies operating retail restaurants comprised the majority of firms that did not have a written code of ethics (40 percent of retail restaurants), and foodservice in lodging operations (37.5 percent) followed them closely. The use of an actively applied code of ethics was found to be greatest in companies with annual sales in excess of $1 billion (90.91 percent). Also, among companies with a large number of operating units, only 12.5 percent of the companies did not have a written code of ethics. Given the growth of the foodservice industry and the potential for abuses, it only seems reasonable that all companies should have and actively apply a code of ethics.

One measure of a company's commitment to minimizing possible ethical dilemmas is through its gift reporting system. Each of the companies in this study reported policies relative to accepting gifts from suppliers. Detailed data regarding those responses by category of organization, annual sales, and number of units in the organization is available in Tables 21a, 21b, and 21c. Most companies with reporting requirements only required a gift to be reported if its value exceeded $25. However, most government institutions require that *all* gifts be reported, *or* insist that *no gifts be accepted*. It appears that as the size of the company increased, by sales or by number of units, gifts valued at less than $25 were acceptable.

Summary And Conclusion

While there is little doubt that most of the purchasing officers maintained similar views on what constitutes very unethical or ethical behavior, purchasing officers in government institutions seemed to possess more definite guidelines for ethics. This is probably due, in part, to the considerable regulations within their operating environment. Also, organizations in the public sector reported very limited occurrence of unethical practices. The category of organization is a significant factor when examining ethical/unethical practices and their frequency of occurrence. It also appears that, as the company increased in size, both in terms of annual sales and in terms of number of operating units, what constituted ethical/unethical practices became more clearly delineated.

It is encouraging that 61.7 percent of the companies that responded had a written code of ethics that is actively applied, but it is somewhat disturbing that 28.4 percent of the companies had only an unwritten code of ethics and the remaining firms had a code of ethics that is not actively applied. Ninety percent of the government institutions responding and over 90 percent of the organizations with annual sales in excess of $1 billion reported having a written code of ethics that is actively applied.

In most companies, only gifts with a value in excess of $25 had to be reported. An exception to this was government institutions, which either disallowed all gifts or required that all gifts be reported.

Given the current size of the industry, projected growth, and the cost of goods sold in the foodservice industry, the matter of ethics in purchasing should be important. The results of this study suggest that, while there is a general consensus on what constitutes ethical behavior, there are still discrepancies of opinion regarding some practices. Furthermore, many of these practices that are considered unethical possibly occur too frequently. It appears that most of the differences are explained by the category of the organization and the size of the organization. Further research should delve into the reasons for these differences.

FUTURE RESEARCH

Given the findings of this exploratory study, future research may yield significant and useful results that would accrue to the management of organizations operating foodservice establishments and the body of knowledge concerning the management of multi-site service operations. Based on the findings of this study, the following areas hold promise for future investigation:

1. *Expanded Sample Size*—Although the sample size of 61 was adequate for drawing conclusions about the foodservice industry generally, it was not sufficient to make definitive statements regarding comparisons of firms based on the category of organization, annual sales, or the number of operating units.

2. *Separate Studies*—Although the data are inclusive, they strongly suggest that lodging operations, institutional operations, and retail restaurants approach purchasing from different perspectives. For example, the hotel firms represented in this sample appeared to push more responsibility for purchasing on local management and appeared to subsume foodservice purchasing under food and beverage operations. Therefore, separate studies of purchasing practices of institutional operations, retail restaurants, and lodging operations would likely produce useful results.

3. *Organizational Relationships*—Although this study gathered data concerning the staffing and operation of the corporate foodservice purchasing department, more research is needed to define organizational relationships. Some possibilities include:
    a. reporting relationships—who reports to purchasing and whom purchasing reports to;
    b. the degree of centralization versus decentralization;
    c. the relationship of purchasing to line management.

4. *Buying Procedures*—Although this study covers a number of buying procedures and criteria, more research is needed. For example, data are needed concerning forecasting methods, bidding procedures, and distribution procedures.

5. *Supplier Evaluation*—Supplier-selection criteria have been delineated but the method and criteria for evaluating supplier performance have not. Further research is needed to ascertain methods and criteria for supplier evaluation as well as to determine what actions are taken with poorly performing suppliers.

6. *Ethics*—The results of this study indicate that there are common occurrences of unethical behavior in

the foodservice industry. A focus of useful future research might deal with substantiating this and establishing why such behavior occurs.

7. *Trends in the Vendor Base*—Although most respondents indicated that they were expanding their vendor base, a substantial number reported that their vendor base had decreased. A possible topic of future research might focus on the rationale for increasing and decreasing vendor bases in the industry as well as on the types of organizations most likely to increase or decrease the number of vendors.

8. *Buyer Performance Evaluation*—Techniques and criteria for evaluating buyer performance need to be investigated.

9. *Career Paths of Chief Purchasing Officers*—Although data have been collected regarding some aspects of CPOs' experience, work is still needed to ascertain what type of experience CPOs have had and how this contributed to their careers.

NOTES

[1] See: R. Dan Reid and Carl D. Riegel, "Purchasing Policy in Multi-Site Foodservice Organizations: An Exploratory Study," in *Proceedings of the 1987 National Purchasing and Materials Management Research Symposium*, ed. Joseph R. Carter and Gary L. Ragatz, National Association of Purchasing Management, 1987; and Carl D. Riegel and R. Dan Reid, "Food-Service Purchasing: Corporate Practices," *The Cornell Hotel and Restaurant Administration Quarterly*, May 1988, pp. 24-29.

[2] See: "The 1987 R and I 400," *Restaurants and Institutions*, Chicago: Cahners Publishing, July 1988.

[3] *Restaurants and Institutions "400" Executive Directory*, Chicago: Cahners Publishing, 1986.

[4] See: Donald W. Dobler, Lamar Lee, Jr., and David N. Burt, *Purchasing and Materials Management: Text and Cases* (New York: McGraw-Hill, 1984), pp. 13-23; and Michiel Leenders, Harold E. Fearon, and Wilbur E. England, *Purchasing and Materials Management* (Homewood, Illinois: Richard D. Irwin, Inc., 1980), pp. 1-27.

[5] Some exceptions include: Al Izzola, "Factors Buyers Consider When Selecting Suppliers," *Hospitality Education and Research Journal*, 8, No. 1 (1984), pp. 51-54; Carl D. Riegel and K. M. Haywood, "Purchasing Attitudes and Behavior in Canadian Foodservice Firms: A Research Note," *Hospitality Education and Research Journal*, 9, No. 1 (1984), pp. 72-82; and R. Dan Reid and Carl D. Riegel, "An Analysis of Supplier-Selection Criteria Importance in the Foodservice Industry: Multi-units versus Single-unit," in *Northeast DSI 1988 Proceedings*, ed. Peter J. Billington, Northeast Region Decision Sciences Institute, 1988.

[6] See: Riegel and Reid.

[7] "Schools Play Favorites with Food Contracts," *Chicago Tribune*, Monday, 13 June 1988, p. 1.

[8] See: Alan J. Dubinsky and John M. Gwin, "Business Ethics: Buyers and Sellers" *Journal of Purchasing and Materials Management*, Winter 1981.

[9] See: William D. Presutti, Jr., "The Ethical Perceptions of Practitioners and Students: A Comparison and Suggestions for Integrating Ethics in Purchasing into the Business School Curriculum" in *Proceedings of the 1987 National Purchasing and Materials Management Research Symposium*, ed. Joseph R. Carter and Gary L. Ragatz, National Association of Purchasing Management, 1987.

TABLE 1a

SIZE OF AVERAGE PURCHASE ORDER BY CATEGORY OF ORGANIZATION

	Private Institution	Government Institution	Retail Restaurant	Foodservice in Lodging
Average purchase order less than $250	0.00%	11.11%	3.70%	0.00%
Average purchase order between $250 and $500	10.00	11.11	7.41	14.29
Average purchase order between $501 and $1,000	30.00	0.00	0.00	28.57
Average purchase order between $1,001 and $2,000	20.00	11.11	14.81	14.29
Average purchase order between $2,001 and $4,000	20.00	11.11	25.93	28.57
Average purchase order between $4,001 and $8,000	0.00	33.33	11.11	14.29
Average purchase order over $8,000	20.00	22.22	37.04	0.00

TABLE 1b

SIZE OF AVERAGE PURCHASE ORDER BY ANNUAL SALES OF ORGANIZATION

	Less than $100 million	$100 million to $1 billion	Greater than $1 billion
Average purchase order less than $250	4.00%	5.88%	0.00%
Average purchase order between $250 and $500	8.00	5.88	20.00
Average purchase order between $501 and 1,000	16.00	5.88	0.00
Average purchase order between $1,001 and $2,000	24.00	5.88	10.00
Average purchase order between $2,001 and $4,000	32.00	23.53	0.00
Average purchase order between $4,001 and $8,000	8.00	17.65	20.00
Average purchase order over $8,000	8.00	35.29	50.00

TABLE 1c

SIZE OF AVERAGE PURCHASE ORDER BY NUMBER OF UNITS IN ORGANIZATION

	Less than 100 units	100 to 249 units	250 to 1,000 units	Greater than 1,000 units
Average purchase order less than $250	4.35%	8.33%	0.00%	0.00%
Average purchase order between $250 and $500	8.70	16.67	11.11	0.00
Average purchase order between $501 and $1,000	8.70	16.67	11.11	0.00
Average purchase order between $1,001 and $2,000	26.09	8.33	11.11	0.00
Average purchase order between $2,001 and $4,000	30.43	25.00	11.11	14.29
Average purchase order between $4,001 and $8,000	13.04	8.33	11.11	14.29
Average purchase order over $8,000	8.70	16.67	44.44	71.43

TABLE 2a

AVERAGE ANNUAL NUMBER OF PURCHASE ORDERS BY CATEGORY OF ORGANIZATION

	Private Institution	Government Institution	Retail Restaurant	Foodservice in Lodging
Average # of P.O.s less than 100	10.00%	0.00%	16.67%	0.00%
Average # of P.O.s between 100 and 250	0.00	0.00	6.67	0.00
Average # of P.O.s between 251 and 500	0.00	10.00	3.33	0.00
Average # of P.O.s between 501 and 1,000	20.00	0.00	10.00	14.29
Average # of P.O.s between 1,001 and 2,000	30.00	20.00	10.00	0.00
Average # of P.O.s between 2,001 and 4,000	10.00	10.00	20.00	0.00
Average # of P.O.s between 4,001 and 8,000	10.00	0.00	10.00	28.57
Average # of P.O.s greater than 8,000	20.00	60.00	23.33	57.14

TABLE 2b

AVERAGE ANNUAL NUMBER OF PURCHASE ORDERS BY ANNUAL SALES OF ORGANIZATION

	Less than $100 million	$100 million to $1 billion	Greater than $1 billion
Average # of P.O.s less than 100	14.29%	11.76%	0.00%
Average # of P.O.s between 100 and 250	7.14	0.00	0.00
Average # of P.O.s between 251 and 500	0.00	5.88	10.00
Average # of P.O.s between 501 and 1,000	10.71	17.65	0.00
Average # of P.O.s between 1,001 and 2,000	14.29	17.65	10.00
Average # of P.O.s between 2,001 and 4,000	7.14	17.65	10.00
Average # of P.O.s between 4,001 and 8,000	17.86	5.88	0.00
Average # of P.O.s greater than 8,000	28.57	23.53	70.00

TABLE 2c

AVERAGE ANNUAL NUMBER OF PURCHASE ORDERS BY NUMBER OF UNITS IN ORGANIZATION

	Less than 100 units	100 to 249 units	250 to 1,000 units	Greater than 1,000 units
Average # of P.O.s less than 100	8.00%	23.08%	0.00%	14.29%
Average # of P.O.s between 100 and 250	8.00	0.00	0.00	0.00
Average # of P.O.s between 251 and 500	4.00	7.69	0.00	0.00
Average # of P.O.s between 501 and 1,000	12.00	7.69	20.00	0.00
Average # of P.O.s between 1,001 and 2,000	16.00	7.69	10.00	28.57
Average # of P.O.s between 2,001 and 4,000	12.00	7.69	20.00	14.29
Average # of P.O.s between 4,001 and 8,000	20.00	7.69	0.00	0.00
Average # of P.O.s greater than 8,000	20.00	38.46	50.00	42.86

TABLE 3a

BUYERS' TRAVEL BY CATEGORY OF ORGANIZATION

	Private Institution	Government Institution	Retail Restaurant	Foodservice in Lodging
Buyers' travel less than 10%	45.45%	90.00%	50.00%	42.86%
Buyers' travel 10 to 29%	54.55	10.00	30.00	28.57
Buyers' travel 30 to 49%	0.00	0.00	13.33	28.57
Buyers' travel 50 to 70%	0.00	0.00	3.33	0.00
Buyers' travel more than 70%	0.00	0.00	3.33	0.00

TABLE 3b

BUYERS' TRAVEL BY ANNUAL SALES OF ORGANIZATION

	Less than $100 million	$100 million to $1 billion	Greater than $1 billion
Buyers' travel less than 10%	68.97%	37.50%	36.36%
Buyers' travel 10 to 29%	17.24	43.75	45.45
Buyers' travel 30 to 49%	6.90	18.75	18.18
Buyers' travel 50 to 70%	3.45	0.00	0.00
Buyers' travel more than 70%	3.45	0.00	0.00

TABLE 3c

BUYERS' TRAVEL BY NUMBER OF UNITS IN ORGANIZATION

	Less than 100 units	100 to 249 units	250 to 1,000 units	Greater than 1,000 units
Buyers' travel less than 10%	70.83%	66.67%	30.00%	0.00%
Buyers' travel 10 to 29%	16.67	20.00	50.00	75.00
Buyers' travel 30 to 49%	8.33	13.33	10.00	25.00
Buyers' travel 50 to 70%	4.17	0.00	0.00	0.00
Buyers' travel more than 70%	0.00	0.00	10.00	0.00

TABLE 4a

DISTRIBUTION OF FORECASTING RESPONSIBILITY BY CATEGORY OF ORGANIZATION

	Private Institution	Government Institution	Retail Restaurant	Foodservice in Lodging
Marketing supplies forecast	10.00%	0.00%	6.67%	0.00%
Operations supplies forecast	10.00	70.00	30.00	62.50
Purchasing supplies forecast	70.00	20.00	60.00	37.50
Forecast from other source	10.00	10.00	3.33	0.00

TABLE 4b

DISTRIBUTION OF FORECASTING RESPONSIBILITY BY ANNUAL SALES OF ORGANIZATION

	Less than $100 million	$100 million to $1 billion	Greater than $1 billion
Marketing supplies forecast	6.90%	5.88%	0.00%
Operations supplies forecast	48.28	29.41	27.27
Purchasing supplies forecast	44.83	58.82	63.64
Forecast from other source	0.00	5.88	9.09

TABLE 4c

DISTRIBUTION OF FORECASTING RESPONSIBILITY BY NUMBER OF UNITS IN ORGANIZATION

	Less than 100 units	100 to 249 units	250 to 1,000 units	Greater than 1,000 units
Marketing supplies forecast	4.00%	7.14%	0.00%	12.50%
Operations supplies forecast	60.00	21.43	30.00	12.50
Purchasing supplies forecast	36.00	57.14	70.00	75.00
Forecast from other source	0.00	14.29	0.00	0.00

TABLE 5a

PURCHASING'S INVOLVEMENT IN STRATEGIC PLANNING BY CATEGORY OF ORGANIZATION

	Private Institution	Government Institution	Retail Restaurant	Foodservice in Lodging
Purchasing completely involved in strategic planning	36.36%	10.00%	50.00%	28.57%
Purchasing somewhat involved in strategic planning	54.55	50.00	36.67	71.43
Purchasing not involved at all in strategic planning	9.09	40.00	13.33	0.00

TABLE 5b

PURCHASING'S INVOLVEMENT IN STRATEGIC PLANNING BY ANNUAL SALES OF ORGANIZATION

	Less than $100 million	$100 million to $1 billion	Greater than $1 billion
Purchasing completely involved in strategic planning	41.38%	37.50%	36.36%
Purchasing somewhat involved in strategic planning	41.38	56.25	45.45
Purchasing not involved at all in strategic planning	17.24	6.25	18.18

TABLE 5c

PURCHASING'S INVOLVEMENT IN STRATEGIC PLANNING BY NUMBER OF UNITS IN ORGANIZATION

	Less than 100 units	100 to 249 units	250 to 1,000 units	Greater than 1,000
Purchasing completely involved in strategic planning	33.33%	33.33%	60.00%	50.00%
Purchasing somewhat involved in strategic planning	45.83	46.67	40.00	50.00
Purchasing not involved at all in strategic planning	20.83	20.00	0.00	0.00

TABLE 6a

ORGANIZATIONAL LEVEL RESPONSIBLE FOR MAKING PURCHASING DECISIONS FOR COMMODITY GROUPS BY CATEGORY OF ORGANIZATION

	Private Institution	Government Institution	Retail Restaurant	Foodservice in Lodging
Meat and Poultry				
Corporate Purchasing	60.00%	40.00%	80.65%	50.00%
Corporate Line Officer	10.00	0.00	9.68	25.00
Regional Staff Mgmt.	0.00	20.00	0.00	0.00
Local Management	30.00	20.00	6.45	25.00
Other	0.00	20.00	3.23	0.00
Produce				
Corporate Purchasing	40.00	10.00	45.16	25.00
Corporate Line Officer	0.00	0.00	6.45	12.50
Regional Staff Mgmt.	10.00	10.00	9.68	0.00
Local Management	30.00	70.00	35.48	50.00
Other	20.00	10.00	3.23	12.50
Dairy Products				
Corporate Purchasing	63.64	30.00	51.61	25.00
Corporate Line Officer	0.00	0.00	3.23	12.50
Regional Staff Mgmt.	0.00	20.00	6.45	0.00
Local Management	18.18	30.00	35.48	50.00
Other	18.18	20.00	3.23	12.50
Groceries				
Corporate Purchasing	60.00	30.00	77.42	62.50
Corporate Line Officer	0.00	0.00	3.23	0.00
Regional Staff Mgmt.	0.00	30.00	6.45	0.00
Local Management	20.00	20.00	9.68	37.50
Other	20.00	20.00	3.23	0.00
Major Equipment				
Corporate Purchasing	72.73	40.00	90.32	50.00
Corporate Line Officer	0.00	10.00	6.45	37.50
Regional Staff Mgmt.	9.09	20.00	3.23	12.50
Local Management	9.09	10.00	0.00	0.00
Other	9.09	20.00	0.00	0.00
Small Wares				
Corporate Purchasing	54.55	20.00	77.42	62.50
Corporate Line Officer	9.09	10.00	0.00	12.50
Regional Staff Mgmt.	0.00	10.00	12.90	0.00
Local Management	27.77	40.00	9.68	25.00
Other	9.09	20.00	0.00	0.00
Nonconsumable Supplies				
Corporate Purchasing	63.64	30.00	80.65	37.50
Corporate Line Officer	9.09	0.00	0.00	25.00
Regional Staff Mgmt.	9.09	10.00	0.00	0.00
Local Management	18.18	40.00	19.35	37.50
Other	0.00	20.00	0.00	0.00

TABLE 6b

ORGANIZATIONAL LEVEL RESPONSIBLE FOR MAKING PURCHASING DECISIONS FOR COMMODITY GROUPS BY ANNUAL SALES OF ORGANIZATION

	Less than $100 million	$100 million to $1 billion	Greater than $1 billion
Meat and Poultry			
Corporate Purchasing	65.52%	76.47%	63.64%
Corporate Line Officer	6.90	11.76	9.09
Regional Staff Mgmt.	3.45	0.00	9.09
Local Management	17.24	11.76	9.09
Other	6.90	0.00	9.09
Produce			
Corporate Purchasing	37.93	47.06	18.18
Corporate Line Officer	3.45	0.00	18.18
Regional Staff Mgmt.	13.79	0.00	9.09
Local Management	37.93	52.94	45.45
Other	6.90	0.00	9.09
Dairy Products			
Corporate Purchasing	51.72	61.11	27.27
Corporate Line Officer	3.45	0.00	9.09
Regional Staff Mgmt.	6.90	0.00	18.18
Local Management	31.03	38.89	27.27
Other	6.90	0.00	18.18
Groceries			
Corporate Purchasing	58.62	82.35	63.64
Corporate Line Officer	3.45	0.00	0.00
Regional Staff Mgmt.	10.34	0.00	18.18
Local Management	20.69	17.65	9.09
Other	6.90	0.00	9.09
Major Equipment			
Corporate Purchasing	72.41	88.89	63.64
Corporate Line Officer	13.79	5.56	9.09
Regional Staff Mgmt.	6.90	5.56	18.18
Local Management	3.45	0.00	0.00
Other	3.45	0.00	9.09
Small Wares			
Corporate Purchasing	55.17	77.78	63.64
Corporate Line Officer	10.34	0.00	0.00
Regional Staff Mgmt.	10.34	5.56	9.09
Local Management	20.69	16.67	18.18
Other	3.45	0.00	9.09
Nonconsumable Supplies			
Corporate Purchasing	62.07	83.33	45.45
Corporate Line Officer	3.45	0.00	9.09
Regional Staff Mgmt.	3.45	0.00	9.09
Local Management	27.59	16.67	27.27
Other	3.45	0.00	9.09

TABLE 6c

ORGANIZATIONAL LEVEL RESPONSIBLE FOR MAKING PURCHASING DECISIONS FOR COMMODITY GROUPS BY NUMBER OF UNITS IN ORGANIZATION

	Less than 100 units	100 to 249 units	250 to 1,000 units	Greater than 1,000 units
Meat and Poultry				
Corporate Purchasing	56.00%	73.33%	72.73%	100.00%
Corporate Line Officer	16.00	6.67	9.09	0.00
Regional Staff Mgmt.	0.00	6.67	9.09	0.00
Local Management	20.00	13.33	0.00	0.00
Other	8.00	0.00	9.09	0.00
Produce				
Corporate Purchasing	40.00	53.33	18.18	28.57
Corporate Line Officer	4.00	0.00	18.18	0.00
Regional Staff Mgmt.	8.00	20.00	0.00	0.00
Local Management	44.00	20.00	54.55	57.14
Other	4.00	6.67	9.09	14.29
Dairy Products				
Corporate Purchasing	44.00	66.67	45.45	37.50
Corporate Line Officer	4.00	0.00	9.09	0.00
Regional Staff Mgmt.	0.00	13.33	9.09	12.50
Local Management	44.00	13.33	27.27	37.50
Other	8.00	6.67	9.09	12.50
Groceries				
Corporate Purchasing	52.00	73.33	81.82	85.71
Corporate Line Officer	4.00	0.00	0.00	0.00
Regional Staff Mgmt.	12.00	6.67	9.09	0.00
Local Management	24.00	13.33	0.00	14.29
Other	8.00	6.67	9.09	0.00
Major Equipment				
Corporate Purchasing	64.00	80.00	90.91	87.50
Corporate Line Officer	16.00	0.00	9.09	12.50
Regional Staff Mgmt.	12.00	13.33	0.00	0.00
Local Management	0.00	0.00	0.00	0.00
Other	8.00	6.67	0.00	0.00
Small Wares				
Corporate Purchasing	52.00	66.67	72.73	87.50
Corporate Line Officer	8.00	0.00	9.09	0.00
Regional Staff Mgmt.	8.00	20.00	0.00	0.00
Local Management	24.00	6.67	18.18	12.50
Other	8.00	6.67	0.00	0.00
Nonconsumable Supplies				
Corporate Purchasing	52.00	73.33	90.91	62.50
Corporate Line Officer	4.00	6.67	0.00	12.50
Regional Staff Mgmt.	4.00	6.67	0.00	0.00
Local Management	32.00	13.33	9.09	25.00
Other	8.00	0.00	0.00	0.00

TABLE 7a

ORGANIZATIONAL LEVEL RESPONSIBLE FOR KEY PURCHASING ACTIVITIES BY CATEGORY OF ORGANIZATION

	Private Institution	Government Institution	Retail Restaurant	Foodservice in Lodging
Recipe development				
Corporate Purchasing	27.27%	0.00%	36.67%	12.50%
Corporate Line Officer	27.27	0.00	36.67	62.50
Regional Staff Mgmt.	0.00	40.00	6.67	12.50
Local Management	27.27	50.00	3.33	12.50
Other	18.18	10.00	16.67	0.00
Menu development				
Corporate Purchasing	27.27	0.00	30.00	12.50
Corporate Line Officer	27.27	10.00	46.67	62.50
Regional Staff Mgmt.	0.00	30.00	10.00	12.50
Local Management	27.27	50.00	0.00	12.50
Other	18.18	10.00	13.33	0.00
Specification writing				
Corporate Purchasing	54.55	40.00	46.67	50.00
Corporate Line Officer	18.18	0.00	30.00	37.50
Regional Staff Mgmt.	0.00	30.00	6.67	0.00
Local Management	27.27	20.00	0.00	12.50
Other	0.00	10.00	16.67	0.00
Approval of buying source				
Corporate Purchasing	63.64	70.00	80.00	50.00
Corporate Line Officer	9.09	0.00	6.67	37.50
Regional Staff Mgmt.	0.00	10.00	0.00	0.00
Local Management	27.27	10.00	0.00	12.50
Other	0.00	10.00	13.33	0.00
Designate approved brands				
Corporate Purchasing	54.55	40.00	53.33	12.50
Corporate Line Officer	9.09	10.00	20.00	62.50
Regional Staff Mgmt.	0.00	30.00	6.67	12.50
Local Management	27.27	10.00	0.00	12.50
Other	9.09	10.00	20.00	0.00
Supplier evaluation				
Corporate Purchasing	63.64	50.00	80.00	50.00
Corporate Line Officer	9.09	10.00	6.67	12.50
Regional Staff Mgmt.	0.00	10.00	3.33	0.00
Local Management	27.27	20.00	10.00	37.50
Other	0.00	10.00	0.00	0.00
Negotiation w/suppliers				
Corporate Purchasing	72.73	66.67	86.67	50.00
Corporate Line Officer	0.00	0.00	0.00	25.00
Regional Staff Mgmt.	9.09	11.11	10.00	0.00
Local Management	18.18	11.11	3.33	25.00
Other	0.00	11.11	0.00	0.00

TABLE 7a (continued)

	Private Institution	Government Institution	Retail Restaurant	Foodservice in Lodging
Change of suppliers				
Corporate Purchasing	63.64%	66.67%	83.33%	50.00%
Corporate Line Officer	9.09	0.00	3.33	25.00
Regional Staff Mgmt.	9.09	11.11	6.67	0.00
Local Management	18.18	11.11	6.67	25.00
Other	0.00	11.11	0.00	0.00
Change of brands				
Corporate Purchasing	45.45	40.00	76.67	12.50
Corporate Line Officer	18.18	10.00	3.33	62.50
Regional Staff Mgmt.	0.00	30.00	10.00	12.50
Local Management	27.27	10.00	0.00	12.50
Other	9.09	10.00	10.00	0.00
Substitute approved brands				
Corporate Purchasing	36.36	40.00	63.33	37.50
Corporate Line Officer	18.18	10.00	3.33	37.50
Regional Staff Mgmt.	9.09	30.00	20.00	12.50
Local Management	27.27	10.00	6.67	12.50
Other	9.09	10.00	6.67	0.00
Approve new products				
Corporate Purchasing	54.55	30.00	46.67	25.00
Corporate Line Officer	9.09	10.00	30.00	50.00
Regional Staff Mgmt.	0.00	20.00	6.67	12.50
Local Management	27.27	30.00	0.00	12.50
Other	9.09	10.00	16.67	0.00
Invoice approval				
Corporate Purchasing	18.18	10.00	36.67	12.50
Corporate Line Officer	9.09	0.00	10.00	25.00
Regional Staff Mgmt.	9.09	30.00	10.00	0.00
Local Management	63.24	60.00	43.33	62.50
Other	0.00	0.00	0.00	0.00
Invoice payment				
Corporate Purchasing	45.45	10.00	50.00	12.50
Corporate Line Officer	18.18	10.00	6.67	37.50
Regional Staff Mgmt.	0.00	30.00	10.00	0.00
Local Management	27.27	50.00	10.00	50.00
Other	9.09	0.00	23.33	0.00
Order placement				
Corporate Purchasing	0.00	50.00	46.67	37.50
Corporate Line Officer	10.00	0.00	3.33	0.00
Regional Staff Mgmt.	10.00	0.00	3.33	0.00
Local Management	80.00	40.00	46.67	62.50
Other	0.00	10.00	0.00	0.00

TABLE 7b

ORGANIZATIONAL LEVEL RESPONSIBLE FOR KEY PURCHASING ACTIVITIES BY ANNUAL SALES OF ORGANIZATION

	Less than $100 million	$100 million to $1 billion	Greater than $1 billion
Recipe development			
Corporate Purchasing	20.69%	41.18%	18.18%
Corporate Line Officer	27.59	41.18	18.18
Regional Staff Mgmt.	13.79	5.88	18.18
Local Management	20.69	0.00	27.27
Other	17.24	11.76	18.18
Menu development			
Corporate Purchasing	17.24	41.18	9.09
Corporate Line Officer	37.93	41.18	27.27
Regional Staff Mgmt.	13.79	5.88	18.18
Local Management	17.24	0.00	27.27
Other	13.79	11.76	18.18
Specification writing			
Corporate Purchasing	48.28	64.71	36.36
Corporate Line Officer	27.59	23.53	9.09
Regional Staff Mgmt.	6.90	0.00	18.18
Local Management	13.79	0.00	9.09
Other	3.45	11.76	27.27
Approval of buying source			
Corporate Purchasing	68.87	82.35	72.73
Corporate Line Officer	13.79	5.88	0.00
Regional Staff Mgmt.	3.45	0.00	0.00
Local Management	10.34	0.00	9.09
Other	3.45	11.76	18.18
Designate approved brands			
Corporate Purchasing	48.28	58.82	27.27
Corporate Line Officer	17.24	23.53	27.27
Regional Staff Mgmt.	13.79	5.88	9.09
Local Management	10.34	0.00	9.09
Other	10.34	11.76	27.27
Supplier evaluation			
Corporate Purchasing	58.62	82.35	72.73
Corporate Line Officer	6.90	5.88	9.09
Regional Staff Mgmt.	6.90	0.00	0.00
Local Management	24.14	11.76	9.09
Other	3.45	0.00	9.09
Negotiation w/suppliers			
Corporate Purchasing	67.86	88.24	81.82
Corporate Line Officer	7.14	0.00	0.00
Regional Staff Mgmt.	14.29	5.88	0.00
Local Management	10.71	5.88	9.09
Other	0.00	0.00	9.09

TABLE 7b (continued)

	Less than $100 million	$100 million to $1 billion	Greater than $1 billion
Change of suppliers			
Corporate Purchasing	64.29%	88.24%	81.82%
Corporate Line Officer	10.71	0.00	0.00
Regional Staff Mgmt.	10.71	5.88	0.00
Local Management	14.29	5.88	9.09
Other	0.00	0.00	9.09
Change of brands			
Corporate Purchasing	55.17	70.59	45.45
Corporate Line Officer	10.34	17.65	18.18
Regional Staff Mgmt.	17.24	5.88	9.09
Local Management	10.34	0.00	9.09
Other	6.90	5.88	18.18
Substitute approved brands			
Corporate Purchasing	44.83	58.82	54.55
Corporate Line Officer	10.34	11.76	9.09
Regional Staff Mgmt.	20.69	23.53	9.09
Local Management	17.24	0.00	9.09
Other	6.90	5.88	18.18
Approve new products			
Corporate Purchasing	41.38	52.94	27.27
Corporate Line Officer	20.69	29.41	27.27
Regional Staff Mgmt.	13.79	5.88	9.09
Local Management	17.24	0.00	9.09
Other	6.90	11.76	27.27
Invoice approval			
Corporate Purchasing	13.79	35.29	27.27
Corporate Line Officer	10.34	11.76	9.09
Regional Staff Mgmt.	13.79	5.88	18.18
Local Management	58.62	47.06	45.45
Other	3.45	0.00	0.00
Invoice payment			
Corporate Purchasing	31.03	64.71	18.18
Corporate Line Officer	13.79	11.76	18.18
Regional Staff Mgmt.	17.24	0.00	9.09
Local Management	31.03	5.88	36.36
Other	6.90	17.65	18.18
Order placement			
Corporate Purchasing	27.59	41.18	54.55
Corporate Line Officer	6.90	0.00	0.00
Regional Staff Mgmt.	0.00	11.76	0.00
Local Management	62.07	47.06	36.36
Other	3.45	0.00	9.09

TABLE 7c

ORGANIZATIONAL LEVEL RESPONSIBLE FOR KEY PURCHASING ACTIVITIES BY NUMBER OF UNITS IN ORGANIZATION

	Less than 100 units	100 to 249 units	250 to 1,000 units	Greater than 1,000 units
Recipe development				
Corporate Purchasing	16.00%	26.67%	50.00%	25.00%
Corporate Line Officer	44.00	20.00	20.00	37.50
Regional Staff Mgmt.	8.00	20.00	20.00	0.00
Local Management	24.00	6.67	10.00	0.00
Other	8.00	26.67	0.00	37.50
Menu development				
Corporate Purchasing	16.00	20.00	40.00	25.00
Corporate Line Officer	52.00	33.33	20.00	37.50
Regional Staff Mgmt.	8.00	13.33	30.00	0.00
Local Management	20.00	6.67	10.00	0.00
Other	4.00	26.67	0.00	37.50
Specification writing				
Corporate Purchasing	44.00	60.00	60.00	37.50
Corporate Line Officer	32.00	20.00	10.00	25.00
Regional Staff Mgmt.	8.00	6.67	20.00	0.00
Local Management	8.00	6.67	10.00	0.00
Other	8.00	6.67	0.00	37.50
Approval of buying source				
Corporate Purchasing	68.00	66.67	90.00	75.00
Corporate Line Officer	16.00	13.33	0.00	0.00
Regional Staff Mgmt.	0.00	6.67	0.00	0.00
Local Management	8.00	6.67	10.00	0.00
Other	8.00	6.67	0.00	25.00
Designate approved brands				
Corporate Purchasing	48.00	40.00	60.00	37.50
Corporate Line Officer	28.00	26.67	0.00	25.00
Regional Staff Mgmt.	8.00	13.33	20.00	0.00
Local Management	8.00	6.67	10.00	0.00
Other	8.00	13.33	10.00	37.50
Supplier evaluation				
Corporate Purchasing	60.00	60.00	70.00	100.00
Corporate Line Officer	8.00	13.33	10.00	0.00
Regional Staff Mgmt.	4.00	0.00	10.00	0.00
Local Management	24.00	20.00	10.00	0.00
Other	4.00	6.67	0.00	0.00
Negotiation w/suppliers				
Corporate Purchasing	64.00	80.00	88.89	100.00
Corporate Line Officer	8.00	0.00	0.00	0.00
Regional Staff Mgmt.	8.00	20.00	0.00	0.00
Local Management	16.00	0.00	11.11	0.00
Other	4.00	0.00	0.00	0.00

TABLE 7c (continued)

	Less than 100 units	100 to 249 units	250 to 1,000 units	Greater than 1,000 units
Change of suppliers				
Corporate Purchasing	68.00%	60.00%	88.89%	100.00%
Corporate Line Officer	8.00	13.33	0.00	0.00
Regional Staff Mgmt.	4.00	20.00	0.00	0.00
Local Management	16.00	6.67	11.11	0.00
Other	4.00	0.00	0.00	0.00
Change of brands				
Corporate Purchasing	52.00	60.00	60.00	62.50
Corporate Line Officer	24.00	13.33	0.00	12.50
Regional Staff Mgmt.	12.00	13.33	20.00	0.00
Local Management	8.00	6.67	10.00	0.00
Other	4.00	6.67	10.00	25.00
Substitute approved brands				
Corporate Purchasing	52.00	26.67	70.00	62.50
Corporate Line Officer	16.00	20.00	0.00	0.00
Regional Staff Mgmt.	16.00	26.67	20.00	12.50
Local Management	12.00	13.33	10.00	0.00
Other	4.00	13.33	0.00	25.00
Approve new products				
Corporate Purchasing	48.00	33.33	50.00	37.50
Corporate Line Officer	28.00	26.67	20.00	25.00
Regional Staff Mgmt.	8.00	13.33	20.00	0.00
Local Management	8.00	13.33	10.00	0.00
Other	8.00	13.33	0.00	37.50
Invoice approval				
Corporate Purchasing	24.00	13.33	40.00	37.50
Corporate Line Officer	12.00	13.33	0.00	12.50
Regional Staff Mgmt.	12.00	13.33	10.00	12.50
Local Management	52.00	53.33	50.00	37.50
Other	0.00	6.67	0.00	0.00
Invoice payment				
Corporate Purchasing	36.00	26.67	60.00	37.50
Corporate Line Officer	12.00	20.00	0.00	25.00
Regional Staff Mgmt.	8.00	13.33	20.00	0.00
Local Management	32.00	20.00	20.00	0.00
Other	12.00	20.00	0.00	37.50
Order placement				
Corporate Purchasing	36.00	21.43	40.00	62.50
Corporate Line Officer	8.00	0.00	0.00	0.00
Regional Staff Mgmt.	0.00	7.14	0.00	12.50
Local Management	52.00	64.29	60.00	25.00
Other	4.00	7.14	0.00	0.00

TABLE 8a

USE OF SPECIFICATIONS BY CATEGORY OF ORGANIZATION

	Private Institution	Government Institution	Retail Restaurant	Foodservice in Lodging
Formal, detailed, written specs	36.36%	80.00%	75.86%	25.00%
Informal, flexible, unwritten specs	9.09	0.00	3.45	25.00
Formal, flexible, written specs	36.36	20.00	10.34	25.00
Somewhere in between	18.18	0.00	10.34	25.00

TABLE 8b

USE OF SPECIFICATIONS BY ANNUAL SALES OF ORGANIZATION

	Less than $100 million	$100 million to $1 billion	Greater than $1 billion
Formal, detailed, written specs	50.00%	70.59%	90.91%
Informal, flexible, unwritten specs	10.71	5.88	0.00
Formal, flexible, written specs	21.43	17.65	9.09
Somewhere in between	17.86	5.88	0.00

TABLE 8c

USE OF SPECIFICATIONS BY NUMBER OF UNITS IN ORGANIZATION

	Less than 100 units	100 to 249 units	250 to 1,000 units	Greater than 1,000
Formal, detailed, written specs	48.00%	57.14%	90.00%	87.50%
Informal, flexible, unwritten specs	16.00	0.00	0.00	0.00
Formal, flexible, written specs	12.00	35.71	10.00	12.50
Somewhere in between	24.00	7.14	0.00	0.00

TABLE 9a

TOTAL NUMBER OF VENDORS USED ANNUALLY BY CATEGORY OF ORGANIZATION

	Private Institution	Government Institution	Retail Restaurant	Foodservice in Lodging
Number of vendors used annually...				
less than 50	9.09%	20.00%	20.00%	12.50%
between 50 and 100	18.18	20.00	26.67	12.50
between 101 and 150	9.09	0.00	10.00	12.50
between 151 and 200	9.09	10.00	0.00	25.00
between 201 and 300	18.18	10.00	10.00	0.00
between 301 and 400	0.00	0.00	10.00	25.00
between 401 and 500	0.00	0.00	13.33	0.00
greater than 500	36.36	40.00	10.00	12.50

TABLE 9b

TOTAL NUMBER OF VENDORS USED ANNUALLY BY ANNUAL SALES OF ORGANIZATION

	Less than $100 million	$100 million to $1 billion	Greater than $1 billion
Number of vendors used annually...			
less than 50	20.69%	23.53%	9.09%
between 50 and 100	31.03	5.88	9.09
between 101 and 150	3.45	17.65	0.00
between 151 and 200	10.34	5.88	0.00
between 201 and 300	10.34	5.88	18.18
between 301 and 400	6.90	11.76	9.09
between 401 and 500	3.45	5.88	18.18
greater than 500	13.79	23.53	36.36

TABLE 9c

TOTAL NUMBER OF VENDORS USED ANNUALLY BY NUMBER OF UNITS IN ORGANIZATION

	Less than 100 units	100 to 249 units	250 to 1,000 units	Greater than 1,000
Number of vendors used annually...				
less than 50	12.00%	26.67%	20.00%	25.00%
between 50 and 100	32.00	20.00	20.00	0.00
between 101 and 150	4.00	6.67	20.00	0.00
between 151 and 200	12.00	0.00	0.00	0.00
between 201 and 300	8.00	6.67	10.00	25.00
between 301 and 400	16.00	0.00	0.00	12.50
between 401 and 500	4.00	6.67	10.00	12.50
greater than 500	12.00	33.33	20.00	25.00

TABLE 10a

USE OF NEW VENDORS BY CATEGORY OF ORGANIZATION

	Private Institution	Government Institution	Retail Restaurant	Foodservice in Lodging
New vendor use has...				
increased significantly	9.09%	20.00%	12.90%	25.00%
increased moderately	63.64	70.00	58.06	62.50
remained constant	18.18	0.00	25.81	12.50
decreased moderately	9.09	10.00	3.23	0.00

TABLE 10b

USE OF NEW VENDORS BY ANNUAL SALES OF ORGANIZATION

	Less than $100 million	$100 million to $1 billion	Greater than $1 billion
New vendor use has...			
increased significantly	10.34%	16.67%	18.18%
increased moderately	62.07	55.56	63.64
remained constant	20.69	22.22	9.09
decreased moderately	6.90	5.56	9.09

TABLE 10c

USE OF NEW VENDORS BY NUMBER OF UNITS IN ORGANIZATION

	Less than 100 units	100 to 249 units	250 to 1,000 units	Greater than 1,000
New vendor use has...				
increased significantly	20.00%	13.33%	0.00%	12.50%
increased moderately	56.00	53.33	63.64	87.50
remained constant	20.00	20.00	27.27	0.00
decreased moderately	4.00	13.33	9.09	0.00

TABLE 11a

TOTAL NUMBER OF VENDORS USED ANNUALLY BY CATEGORY OF ORGANIZATION

	Private Institution	Government Institution	Retail Restaurant	Foodservice in Lodging
Total number of vendors used has...				
increased at a high rate	9.09%	20.00%	12.90%	12.50%
increased moderately	54.55	60.00	58.06	87.50
decreased moderately	27.27	10.00	25.81	0.00
decreased significantly	9.09	10.00	3.23	0.00

TABLE 11b

TOTAL NUMBER OF VENDORS USED ANNUALLY BY ANNUAL SALES OF ORGANIZATION

	Less than $100 million	$100 million to $1 billion	Greater than $1 billion
Total number of vendors used has...			
increased at a high rate	6.90%	16.67%	18.18%
increased moderately	58.62	55.56	81.82
decreased moderately	31.03	16.67	0.00
decreased significantly	3.45	11.11	0.00

TABLE 11c

TOTAL NUMBER OF VENDORS USED ANNUALLY BY NUMBER OF UNITS IN ORGANIZATION

	Less than 100 units	100 to 249 units	250 to 1,000 units	Greater than 1,000
Total number of vendors used has...				
increased at a high rate	16.00%	13.33%	0.00%	12.50%
increased moderately	52.00	53.33	90.91	75.00
decreased moderately	32.00	26.67	9.09	0.00
decreased significantly	0.00	6.67	0.00	12.50

TABLE 12a

USE OF INTERNATIONAL VENDORS BY CATEGORY OF ORGANIZATION

	Private Institution	Government Institution	Retail Restaurant	Foodservice in Lodging
International vendor use has...				
increased significantly	0.00%	10.00%	3.45%	12.50%
increased gradually	36.36	20.00	51.72	25.00
decreased gradually	9.09	20.00	3.45	12.50
decreased significantly	9.09	0.00	3.45	0.00
none used	45.45	50.00	37.93	50.00

TABLE 12b

USE OF INTERNATIONAL VENDORS BY ANNUAL SALES OF ORGANIZATION

	Less than $100 million	$100 million to $1 billion	Greater than $1 billion
International vendor use has...			
increased significantly	3.57%	5.88%	9.09%
increased gradually	28.57	35.29	54.55
decreased gradually	10.71	5.88	9.09
decreased significantly	0.00	11.76	0.00
none used	57.14	41.18	27.27

TABLE 12c

USE OF INTERNATIONAL VENDORS BY NUMBER OF UNITS IN ORGANIZATION

	Less than 100 units	100 to 249 units	250 to 1,000 units	Greater than 1,000
International vendor use has...				
increased significantly	8.00%	0.00%	0.00%	12.50%
increased gradually	28.00	40.00	44.44	62.50
decreased gradually	12.00	0.00	11.11	0.00
decreased significantly	0.00	6.67	11.11	0.00
none used	52.00	53.33	33.33	25.00

TABLE 13a

SITE VISITATION TO VENDORS BY CATEGORY OF ORGANIZATION

	Private Institution	Government Institution	Retail Restaurant	Foodservice in Lodging
Percentage of suppliers visited annually...				
less than 10%	81.82%	80.00%	41.94%	50.00%
between 10 and 24%	0.00	10.00	22.58	12.50
between 25 and 49%	0.00	10.00	9.68	25.00
between 50 and 75%	18.18	0.00	9.68	0.00
more than 75%	0.00	0.00	16.13	12.50

TABLE 13b

SITE VISITATION TO VENDORS BY ANNUAL SALES OF ORGANIZATION

	Less than $100 million	$100 million to $1 billion	Greater than $1 billion
Percentage of suppliers visited annually...			
less than 10%	65.52%	44.44%	36.36%
between 10 and 24%	3.45	33.33	18.18
between 25 and 49%	10.34	11.11	9.09
between 50 and 75%	10.34	5.56	9.09
more than 75%	10.34	5.56	27.27

TABLE 13c

SITE VISITATION TO VENDORS BY NUMBER OF UNITS IN ORGANIZATION

	Less than 100 units	100 to 249 units	250 to 1,000 units	Greater than 1,000
Percentage of suppliers visited annually...				
less than 10%	60.00%	66.67%	54.55%	12.50%
between 10 and 24%	12.00	0.00	18.18	50.00
between 25 and 49%	16.00	6.67	9.09	0.00
between 50 and 75%	4.00	13.33	9.09	12.50
more than 75%	8.00	13.33	9.09	25.00

TABLE 14a

USE OF SINGLE SOURCE SUPPLIERS BY CATEGORY OF ORGANIZATION

	Private Institution	Government Institution	Retail Restaurant	Foodservice in Lodging
Single source suppliers are used...				
only when no other source is available	36.36%	80.00%	23.33%	75.00%
only for standard items which can be easily bought elsewhere	9.09	0.00	10.00	0.00
only for proprietary items	36.36	20.00	46.67	12.50
other	18.18	0.00	20.00	12.50

TABLE 14b

USE OF SINGLE SOURCE SUPPLIERS BY ANNUAL SALES OF ORGANIZATION

	Less than $100 million	$100 million to $1 billion	Greater than $1 billion
Single source suppliers are used...			
only when no other option is available	37.93%	44.44%	50.00%
only for standard items which can be easily bought elsewhere	10.34	5.56	0.00
only for proprietary items	34.48	33.33	30.00
other	17.24	16.67	20.00

TABLE 14c

USE OF SINGLE SOURCE SUPPLIERS BY NUMBER OF UNITS IN ORGANIZATION

	Less than 100 units	100 to 249 units	250 to 1,000 units	Greater than 1,000 units
Single source suppliers are used...				
only when no other option is available	40.00%	33.33%	36.36%	57.14%
only for standard items which can be easily bought elsewhere	16.00	0.00	0.00	0.00
only for proprietary items	32.00	46.67	36.36	28.57
other	12.00	20.00	27.27	14.29

TABLE 15a

SOURCE FOR COMMODITIES BY CATEGORY OF ORGANIZATION

	Private Institution	Government Institution	Retail Restaurant	Foodservice in Lodging
Meat and Poultry				
Corporate Commissary/Warehouse	11.11%	20.00%	29.03%	12.50%
National Vendor	33.33	20.00	35.48	50.00
Regional Vendor	22.22	20.00	22.58	12.50
Local Vendor	33.33	30.00	12.90	25.00
Other	0.00	10.00	0.00	0.00
Produce				
Corporate Commissary/Warehouse	0.00	10.00	10.00	0.00
Nation Vendor	11.11	0.00	0.00	12.50
Regional Vendor	22.22	10.00	23.33	12.50
Local Vendor	66.67	70.00	63.33	75.00
Other	0.00	10.00	3.33	0.00
Dairy Products				
Corporate Commissary/Warehouse	0.00	10.00	12.90	0.00
National Vendor	10.00	10.00	6.45	25.00
Regional Vendor	50.00	40.00	22.58	12.50
Local Vendor	40.00	30.00	58.06	62.50
Other	0.00	10.00	0.00	0.00
Groceries				
Corporate Commisary/Warehouse	0.00	20.00	25.82	0.00
National Vendor	22.22	30.00	45.16	50.00
Regional Vendor	33.33	20.00	16.13	25.00
Local Vendor	44.44	20.00	9.68	25.00
Other	0.00	10.00	3.23	0.00
Major Equipment				
Corporate Commissary/Warehouse	0.00	10.00	22.58	0.00
National Vendor	80.00	50.00	58.06	62.50
Regional Vendor	10.00	20.00	16.13	12.50
Local Vendor	10.00	10.00	3.23	12.50
Other	0.00	10.00	0.00	12.50
Small Wares				
Corporate Commissary/Warehouse	0.00	20.00	22.58	0.00
National Vendor	60.00	10.00	45.16	25.00
Regional Vendor	10.00	30.00	29.03	25.00
Local Vendor	30.00	30.00	3.23	50.00
Other	0.00	10.00	0.00	0.00
Nonconsumable Supplies				
Corporate Commissary/Warehouse	0.00	10.00	25.81	0.00
National Vendor	30.00	20.00	45.16	50.00
Regional Vendor	40.00	20.00	12.90	0.00
Local Vendor	20.00	40.00	16.13	37.50
Other	10.00	10.00	0.00	12.50

TABLE 15b

SOURCE FOR COMMODITIES BY ANNUAL SALES OF ORGANIZATION

	Less than $100 million	$100 million to $1 billion	Greater than $1 billion
Meat and Poultry			
Corporate Commissary/Warehouse	10.34%	23.53%	45.45%
National Vendor	27.59	35.29	45.45
Regional Vendor	27.59	29.41	0.00
Local Vendor	31.03	11.76	9.09
Other	3.45	0.00	0.00
Produce			
Corporate Commissary/Warehouse	6.90	6.25	9.09
Nation Vendor	3.45	0.00	9.09
Regional Vendor	20.69	31.25	9.09
Local Vendor	65.52	56.25	72.73
Other	3.45	6.25	0.00
Dairy Products			
Corporate Commissary/Warehouse	6.90	11.11	9.09
National Vendor	3.45	16.67	18.18
Regional Vendor	37.93	27.78	9.09
Local Vendor	48.28	44.44	63.64
Other	3.45	0.00	0.00
Groceries			
Corporate Commisary/Warehouse	6.90	11.76	45.45
National Vendor	37.93	47.06	45.45
Regional Vendor	24.14	29.41	0.00
Local Vendor	24.14	11.76	9.09
Other	6.90	0.00	0.00
Major Equipment			
Corporate Commissary/Warehouse	10.34	11.11	27.27
National Vendor	58.62	77.78	45.45
Regional Vendor	20.09	5.56	9.09
Local Vendor	6.90	5.56	9.09
Other	3.45	0.00	9.09
Small Wares			
Corporate Commissary/Warehouse	10.34	11.11	36.36
National Vendor	34.48	61.11	18.18
Regional Vendor	37.93	11.11	9.09
Local Vendor	13.79	16.67	36.36
Other	3.45	0.00	0.00
Nonconsumable Supplies			
Corporate Commissary/Warehouse	6.90	11.11	36.36
National Vendor	41.38	50.00	27.27
Regional Vendor	17.24	27.78	0.00
Local Vendor	31.03	11.11	27.27
Other	3.45	0.00	9.09

TABLE 15c

SOURCE FOR COMMODITIES BY NUMBER OF UNITS IN ORGANIZATION

	Less than 100 units	100 to 249 units	250 to 1,000 units	Greater than 1,000
Meat and Poultry				
Corporate Commissary/Warehouse	16.00%	14.29%	36.36%	28.57%
National Vendor	28.00	14.29	45.45	71.73
Regional Vendor	28.00	35.71	9.09	0.00
Local Vendor	28.00	28.57	9.09	0.00
Other	0.00	7.14	0.00	0.00
Produce				
Corporate Commissary/Warehouse	0.00	14.29	0.00	14.29
Nation Vendor	4.00	0.00	10.00	0.00
Regional Vendor	24.00	21.43	20.00	14.29
Local Vendor	72.00	50.00	70.00	71.43
Other	0.00	14.29	0.00	0.00
Dairy Products				
Corporate Commissary/Warehouse	0.00	14.29	9.09	12.50
National Vendor	12.00	0.00	18.18	12.50
Regional Vendor	40.00	28.57	18.18	12.50
Local Vendor	48.00	50.00	54.55	62.50
Other	0.00	7.14	0.00	0.00
Groceries				
Corporate Commisary/Warehouse	8.00	14.29	27.27	28.57
National Vendor	40.00	28.57	45.45	71.43
Regional Vendor	24.00	28.57	18.18	0.00
Local Vendor	24.00	21.43	9.09	0.00
Other	4.00	7.14	0.00	0.00
Major Equipment				
Corporate Commissary/Warehouse	4.00	14.29	18.18	25.00
National Vendor	56.00	57.14	72.73	75.00
Regional Vendor	32.00	7.14	0.00	0.00
Local Vendor	8.00	14.29	0.00	0.00
Other	0.00	7.14	9.09	0.00
Small Wares				
Corporate Commissary/Warehouse	0.00	21.43	27.27	25.00
National Vendor	36.00	42.86	36.36	50.00
Regional Vendor	44.00	7.14	9.09	25.00
Local Vendor	20.00	21.43	27.27	0.00
Other	0.00	7.14	0.00	0.00
Nonconsumable Supplies				
Corporate Commissary/Warehouse	4.00	14.29	27.27	25.00
National Vendor	40.00	35.71	36.36	62.50
Regional Vendor	20.00	21.43	9.09	12.50
Local Vendor	36.00	21.43	18.18	0.00
Other	0.00	7.14	9.09	0.00

TABLE 16a

SUPPLIER-SELECTION CRITERIA BY CATEGORY OF ORGANIZATION

	Private Institution	Government Institution	Retail Restaurant	Foodservice in Lodging
Accuracy in filling orders	1.11%	1.13%	1.21%	1.14%
Consistent quality level	1.11	1.13	1.14	1.43
On-time delivery	1.33	1.13	1.28	1.10
Willingness to work on resolving problems	1.33	1.50	1.24	1.71
Willingness to respond in a "pinch"	1.44	1.75	1.55	1.29
Reasonable unit cost	1.78	1.75	1.52	1.57
Reasonable lead times	1.67	1.88	2.11	2.14
Frequency of delivery	1.44	1.50	2.48	2.00
Technical competence	1.88	1.50	2.28	2.29
Lowest unit cost	2.11	2.25	2.17	2.00
Reasonable payment policy	1.89	2.75	2.41	1.71
Volume discounts	1.55	2.88	2.59	1.14
Knowledgeable sales staff	2.00	2.13	2.41	2.57
Reasonable minimum order	1.55	2.25	2.96	2.43
Geographical distance	2.13	2.50	2.72	3.43
Prompt payment discounts	2.22	3.25	2.83	2.14
Ability to be single source	2.13	3.88	3.21	3.57
Training in product use	2.55	2.63	3.72	3.00
Willing to break a case	3.11	3.75	3.93	3.14
Provision of recipe ideas	2.67	3.43	4.31	3.86

TABLE 16b

SUPPLER-SELECTION CRITERIA BY ANNUAL SALES OF ORGANIZATION

	Less than $100 million	$100 million to $1 billion	Greater than $1 billion
Accuracy in filling orders	1.08%	1.18%	1.36%
Consistent quality level	1.20	1.18	1.09
On-time delivery	1.20	1.24	1.27
Willingness to work on resolving problems	1.16	1.59	1.45
Willingness to respond in a "pinch"	1.60	1.65	1.18
Reasonable unit cost	1.64	1.59	1.55
Reasonable lead times	2.00	2.06	1.91
Frequency of delivery	2.00	2.06	2.36
Technical competence	2.24	2.18	1.64
Lowest unit cost	2.28	2.00	2.09
Reasonable payment policy	2.32	2.18	2.36
Volume discounts	2.36	2.18	2.36
Knowledgeable sales staff	2.12	2.94	2.82

TABLE 16b (continued)

	Less than $100 million	$100 million to $1 billion	Greater than $1 billion
Reasonable minimum order	2.28%	2.65%	3.00%
Geographical distance	2.63	2.76	2.73
Prompt payment discounts	2.80	2.76	2.36
Ability to be sole source	3.00	3.18	3.82
Training in product use	3.12	3.47	3.27
Willing to break a case	3.44	3.94	3.73
Provision of recipe ideas	3.68	4.18	3.70

TABLE 16c

SUPPLIER-SELECTION CRITERIA BY NUMBER OF UNITS IN ORGANIZATION

	Less than 100 units	100 to 249 units	250 to 1,000 units	Greater than 1,000 units
Accuracy in filling orders	1.23%	1.08%	1.10%	1.25%
Consistent quality level	1.32	1.00	1.20	1.00
On-time delivery	1.23	1.31	1.30	1.00
Willingness to work on resolving problems	1.55	1.08	1.40	1.25
Willingness to respond in a "pinch"	1.59	1.69	1.50	1.13
Reasonable unit cost	1.59	1.62	1.50	1.75
Reasonable lead times	1.81	2.15	2.40	2.13
Frequency of delivery	2.14	1.77	2.40	2.13
Technical competence	2.27	2.15	1.90	1.75
Lowest unit cost	2.45	1.92	2.30	1.50
Reasonable payment policy	2.27	2.15	2.80	1.88
Volume discounts	2.32	2.23	2.70	1.88
Knowledgeable sales staff	2.09	2.15	2.80	2.63
Reasonable minimum order	2.55	2.38	2.60	2.00
Geographical distance	3.00	2.58	2.80	1.88
Prompt payment discounts	2.91	2.85	2.60	2.00
Ability to be sole source	3.05	3.15	3.70	3.25
Training in product use	3.27	3.00	3.10	3.88
Willing to break a case	3.45	3.62	3.90	4.00
Provision of recipe ideas	3.95	3.54	4.00	3.88

TABLE 17a

METHODS FOR ASSURING ON-TIME DELIVERY BY CATEGORY OF ORGANIZATION

	Private Institution	Government Institution	Retail Restaurant	Foodservice in Lodging
Develop a good vendor relationship	1.13%	2.25%	1.10%	1.13%
Use your purchasing clout	1.78	2.25	1.50	1.25
Use multiple sources	2.11	2.13	2.25	2.00
Negotiate long-term contracts with performance clauses	2.55	2.00	2.97	1.88
Use exclusivity contracts	2.11	3.38	2.79	2.13
Pay a somewhat higher unit price	3.22	4.00	3.79	4.00
Provide corporate incentives	3.88	3.75	4.55	4.25

TABLE 17b

METHODS FOR ASSURING ON-TIME DELIVERY BY ANNUAL SALES OF ORGANIZATION

	Less than $100 million	$100 million to $1 billion	Greater than $1 billion
Develop a good vendor relationship	1.35%	1.24%	1.40%
Use your purchasing clout	1.62	1.81	1.36
Use multiple sources	2.42	2.00	1.80
Negotiate long-term contracts with performance clauses	2.54	2.88	2.27
Use exclusivity contracts	2.65	2.35	3.18
Pay a somewhat higher unit price	3.54	3.88	4.09
Provide corporate incentives	4.27	4.47	4.00

TABLE 17c

METHODS FOR ASSURING ON-TIME DELIVERY BY NUMBER OF UNITS IN ORGANIZATION

	Less than 100 units	100 to 249 units	250 to 1,000 units	Greater than 1,000 units
Develop a good vendor relationship	1.26%	1.46%	1.56%	1.00%
Use your purchasing clout	1.57	2.08	1.33	1.38
Use multiple sources	2.22	2.38	2.11	1.75
Negotiate long-term contracts with performance clauses	2.83	2.23	2.50	2.03
Use exclusivity contracts	2.87	2.38	3.00	2.13
Pay a somewhat higher unit price	3.61	3.77	4.10	3.75
Provide corporate incentives	4.30	3.92	4.60	4.38

TABLE 18a

MEAN SCORE OF PERCEPTIONS OF ETHICAL DILEMMAS BY CATEGORY OF ORGANIZATION

	Private Institution	Government Institution	Retail Restaurant	Foodservice in Lodging
Gaining information about competitor from your supplier	2.89%	2.38%	3.21%	2.50%
Allowing physical gifts	1.33	1.11	1.97	1.25
Overstating seriousness of problem	1.33	1.44	1.83	2.00
Preference to suppliers favored by top mgmt.	1.44	1.22	2.27	2.38
Preference to suppliers who are good customers	1.89	2.00	2.83	3.13
Allowing free trips, entertainment, etc.	2.44	1.22	2.62	2.25
Allowing personalities to enter into decision	2.67	1.33	2.82	2.13
Allowing info on quotes	1.22	1.00	1.61	2.00
Bias against companies short-cutting purchasing dept.	3.33	1.78	2.86	2.75
Threatening to use second source	3.55	3.33	3.86	4.38
Using firm's economic clout	5.00	4.00	4.89	4.88

TABLE 18b

MEAN SCORE OF PERCEPTIONS OF ETHICAL DILEMMAS BY ANNUAL SALES OF ORGANIZATION

	Less than $100 million	$100 million to $1 billion	Greater than $1 billion
Gaining information about competitor from your supplier	2.92%	3.00%	2.82%
Allowing physical gifts	1.74	1.59	1.36
Overstating seriousness of problem	1.56	2.00	1.64
Preference to suppliers favored by top mgmt.	1.96	2.11	1.82
Preference to suppliers who are good customers	2.83	2.33	2.55
Allowing free trips, entertainment, etc.	2.12	2.89	1.82
Allowing personalities to enter into decision	2.77	2.29	1.91
Allowing info on quotes	1.73	1.35	1.18
Bias against companies short-cutting purchasing dept.	2.93	2.76	2.27
Threatening to use second source	3.69	3.65	4.27
Using firm's economic clout	4.81	4.88	4.82

TABLE 18c

MEAN SCORE OF PERCEPTIONS OF ETHICAL DILEMMAS BY NUMBER OF UNITS IN ORGANIZATION

	Less than 100 units	100 to 249 units	250 to 1,000 units	Greater than 1,000 units
Gaining information about competitor from your supplier	3.13%	1.71%	2.80%	2.88%
Allowing physical gifts	1.71	1.54	1.90	1.13
Overstating seriousness of problem	1.71	1.62	2.00	1.50
Preference to suppliers favored by top mgmt.	2.29	1.38	1.82	2.25
Preference to suppliers who are good customers	3.13	1.92	2.00	2.88
Allowing free trips, entertainment, etc.	2.21	2.17	3.09	1.75
Allowing personalities to enter into decision	2.67	2.09	2.55	2.13
Allowing info on quotes	1.83	1.33	1.10	1.25
Bias against companies short-cutting purchasing dept.	2.88	2.92	2.80	2.00
Threatening to use second source	3.92	3.58	3.50	4.13
Using firm's economic clout	4.83	4.75	4.80	5.00

TABLE 19a

PERCEPTIONS ON FREQUENCY OF OCCURRENCE OF INDUSTRY BEHAVIORS BY CATEGORY OF ORGANIZATION

	Private Institution	Government Institution	Retail Restaurant	Foodservice in Lodging
Gaining information about competitor from your supplier	2.67%	2.86%	2.24%	2.75%
Allowing physical gifts	2.88	4.00	2.69	2.50
Overstating seriousness of problem	2.44	3.63	2.52	3.00
Preference to suppliers favored by top mgmt.	3.11	4.25	2.90	2.88
Preference to suppliers who are good customers	3.33	4.43	3.00	3.00
Allowing free trips, entertainment, etc.	2.33	4.00	2.70	3.13
Allowing personalities to enter into decision	2.78	4.13	2.60	3.25
Allowing info on quotes	3.11	4.13	3.07	3.00
Bias against companies short-cutting purchasing dept.	2.89	4.14	3.07	2.88
Threatening to use second source	2.33	2.88	2.07	2.00
Using firm's economic clout	1.44	2.00	1.13	1.50

TABLE 19b

PERCEPTIONS ON FREQUENCY OF OCCURRENCE
OF INDUSTRY BEHAVIORS BY ANNUAL SALES OF ORGANIZATION

	Less than $100 million	$100 million to $1 billion	Greater than $1 billion
Gaining information about competitor from your supplier	2.40%	2.47%	2.64%
Allowing physical gifts	2.85	3.12	2.64
Overstating seriousness of problem	2.62	3.00	2.64
Preference to suppliers favored by top mgmt.	2.92	2.94	3.91
Preference to suppliers who are good customers	2.96	3.39	3.64
Allowing free trips, entertainment, etc.	2.85	2.72	3.27
Allowing personalities to enter into decision	2.69	2.89	3.64
Allowing info on quotes	3.08	3.50	3.73
Bias against companies short-cutting purchasing dept.	2.84	3.33	3.55
Threatening to use second source	2.08	2.22	2.55
Using firm's economic clout	1.35	1.39	1.36

TABLE 19c

PERCEPTIONS ON FREQUENCY OF OCCURRENCE
OF INDUSTRY BEHAVIORS BY NUMBER OF UNITS IN ORGANIZATION

	Less than 100 units	100 to 249 units	250 to 1,000 units	Greater than 1,000 units
Gaining information about competitor from your supplier	2.35%	2.69%	2.78%	2.13%
Allowing physical gifts	2.96	3.08	3.00	2.25
Overstating seriousness of problem	2.74	3.00	2.70	2.38
Preference to suppliers favored by top mgmt.	2.83	3.50	3.73	2.63
Preference to suppliers who are good customers	2.87	3.77	3.90	2.63
Allowing free trips, entertainment, etc.	3.30	2.69	2.45	2.63
Allowing personalities to enter into decision	2.96	2.85	3.18	2.75
Allowing info on quotes	3.22	3.31	3.90	3.13
Bias against companies short-cutting purchasing dept.	3.04	3.08	3.80	2.75
Threatening to use second source	2.00	2.38	2.64	2.00
Using firm's economic clout	1.35	1.31	1.55	1.25

TABLE 20a

USE OF CODE OF ETHICS BY CATEGORY OF ORGANIZATION

	Private Institution	Government Institution	Retail Restaurant	Foodservice in Lodging
Code of ethics is...				
actively applied	72.73%	90.00%	50.00%	62.50%
used occasionally	9.09	0.00	10.00	0.00
not monitored	0.00	10.00	0.00	0.00
not written	18.18	0.00	40.00	37.50

TABLE 20b

USE OF CODE OF ETHICS BY ANNUAL SALES OF ORGANIZATION

	Less than $100 million	$100 million to $1 billion	Greater than $1 billion
Code of ethics is...			
actively applied	55.17%	52.94%	90.91%
used occasionally	0.00	17.65	0.00
not monitored	6.90	0.00	0.00
not written	38.93	29.41	9.09

TABLE 20c

USE OF CODE OF ETHICS BY NUMBER OF UNITS IN ORGANIZATION

	Less than 100 units	100 to 249 units	250 to 1,000 units	Greater than 1,000 units
Code of ethics is...				
actively applied	60.00%	53.33%	60.00%	75.00%
used occasionally	0.00	13.33	10.00	12.50
not monitored	0.00	6.67	10.00	0.00
not written	40.00	26.67	20.00	12.50

TABLE 21a

GIFT REPORTING REQUIREMENTS BY CATEGORY OF ORGANIZATION

	Private Institution	Government Institution	Retail Restaurant	Foodservice in Lodging
Reporting of gifts from suppliers...				
All gifts reported	36.36%	42.86%	20.00%	42.86%
No reporting if gift value less than $25	63.64	14.29	70.00	57.14
Other responses	0.00	42.85	10.00	0.00

TABLE 21b

GIFT REPORTING REQUIREMENTS BY ANNUAL SALES OF ORGANIZATION

	Less than $100 million	$100 million to $1 billion	Greater than $1 billion
Reporting of gifts from suppliers...			
All gifts reported	40.00%	17.65%	27.27%
No reporting if gift value less than $25	44.00	82.35	54.55
Other responses	16.00	0.00	18.08

TABLE 21c

GIFT REPORTING REQUIREMENTS BY NUMBER OF UNITS IN ORGANIZATION

	Less than 100 units	100 to 249 units	250 to 1,000 units	Greater than 1,000 units
Reporting of gifts from suppliers...				
All gifts reported	39.13%	30.77%	10.00%	12.50%
No reporting if gift value less than $25	47.83	61.54	80.00	75.00
Other responses	13.04	7.69	10.00	12.50

APPENDIX

FOODSERVICE PURCHASING QUESTIONNAIRE

QUESTIONS ONE THROUGH FIVE CONCERN THE TYPE AND SCALE OF YOUR FOODSERVICE OPERATIONS. ALL RESPONSES WILL BE HELD IN STRICT CONFIDENCE.

Please circle the letter of the most appropriate response.

1. Which of the following terms best describes your company?

    a. Private Institutional Foodservice
    b. Government Institutional Foodservice
    c. Retail Restaurant
    d. Foodservice in Lodging

2. Does your company act...

    a. Primarily as a franchiser
    b. Primarily as an operator of company-owned units
    c. Not applicable

3. Which of the following ranges best describes your annual foodservice sales?

    a. Less than $100 million
    b. Between $100 and $299 million
    c. Between $300 and $499 million
    d. Between $500 and $999 million
    e. Between $1 and $1.99 billion
    f. Between $2 and $2.99 billion
    g. Between $3 and $5.99 billion
    h. Greater than $5.99 billion

4. Which of the following ranges best describes the average food and beverage sales of individual units in your company?

    a. Less than $500,000
    b. Between $500,000 and $999,999
    c. Between $1 and $1.49 million
    d. Between $1.5 and $1.99 million
    e. Between $2 and $2.49 million
    f. Greater than $2.49 million

5. Which of the following ranges best identifies the total number of operating units in your company?

    a. Less than 100
    b. Between 100 and 249
    c. Between 250 and 499
    d. Between 500 and 999
    e. Between 1,000 and 1,999
    f. Between 2,000 and 2,999
    g. More than 2,999

QUESTIONS 6 THROUGH 13 ARE CONCERNED WITH THE WAY YOUR PURCHASING DEPARTMENT FUNCTIONS...

6. How many employees work within the purchasing department in your company?

    _____

7. How many of the employees within the purchasing department are buyers or purchasing agents?

   _____

8. Please indicate how buyers are assigned their areas of responsibility.

   a. By commodity groups
   b. By geographical regions
   c. By other means (Please specify) _____

9. Which of the following responses best indicates the percentage of time your buyers are traveling?

   a. Less than 10%
   b. At least 10% but less than 30%
   c. At least 30% but less than 50%
   d. At least 50% but less than 70%
   e. 70% or greater

10. Which department listed below has the primary responsibility for forecasting product needs?

    a. Marketing
    b. Operations
    c. Purchasing
    d. Other (Please specify) _____

11. How involved is your purchasing department in organizational strategic planning?

    a. Completely involved in the process
    b. Somewhat involved in the process
    c. Not involved at all in the process

12. Please indicate which range best reflects the average size of a purchase order from your company.

    a. Less than $250
    b. Between $250 and $500
    c. Between $501 and $1,000
    d. Between $1,001 and $2,000
    e. Between $2,001 and $4,000
    f. Between $4,001 and $8,000
    g. Greater than $8,000

13. Please indicate which range best reflects the average number of purchase orders your company issues each year.

    a. Less than 100
    b. Between 100 and 250
    c. Between 251 and 500
    d. Between 501 and 1,000
    e. Between 1,001 and 2,000
    f. Between 2,001 and 4,000
    g. Between 4,001 and 8,000
    h. Greater than 8,000

QUESTIONS 14 THROUGH 23 CONCERN THE DISTRIBUTION OF ACTIVITIES AND RESPONSIBILITIES WITHIN YOUR FIRM...

14. While the corporate purchasing staff, corporate line managers, regional operations staff, and local managers share responsibility for the following purchase decisions, the level at which decisions are made varies from firm to firm. Listed below are product decision areas which may vary.

Please indicate which level has PRIMARY responsibility for the commodities listed below.

	Corporate Purchasing Office	Corporate Line Officer	Regional Staff Mgmt.	Local Mgmt.	Other (please specify)
Meat and Poultry	1	2	3	4	5
Produce	1	2	3	4	5
Dairy Products	1	2	3	4	5
Groceries	1	2	3	4	5
Major Equipment	1	2	3	4	5
Small Wares	1	2	3	4	5
Nonconsumable Supplies	1	2	3	4	5

15. Please circle your primary source for each of the following purchased items.

	Corporate-Owned Commissary or Warehouse	Approved National Vendor	Approved Regional Vendor	Approved Local Vendor	Other (please specify)
Meat and Poultry	1	2	3	4	5
Produce	1	2	3	4	5
Dairy Products	1	2	3	4	5
Groceries	1	2	3	4	5
Major Equipment	1	2	3	4	5
Small Wares	1	2	3	4	5
Nonconsumable Supplies	1	2	3	4	5

16. Which of the following best describes how invoices are paid in your company?

   a. At the corporate level
   b. At the local level
   c. Other (please specify) _____

17. The activities listed below are typically performed at different levels in different companies. Please indicate the level in your company which has PRIMARY responsibility for performing each activity.

		Level of Responsibility				
		Corporate Purchasing Office	Corporate Line Officer	Regional Staff Mgmt.	Local Mgmt.	Other
a.	Recipe development	1	2	3	4	5
b.	Menu development	1	2	3	4	5
c.	Specification writing	1	2	3	4	5
d.	Approval of buying source	1	2	3	4	5
e.	Designation of approved brands	1	2	3	4	5
f.	Supplier evaluation	1	2	3	4	5
g.	Negotiation with suppliers	1	2	3	4	5
h.	Change of suppliers	1	2	3	4	5
i.	Change of brands	1	2	3	4	5
j.	Substitution of approved items	1	2	3	4	5
k.	Approve new products	1	2	3	4	5
l.	Invoice approval	1	2	3	4	5
m.	Invoice payment	1	2	3	4	5
n.	Order placement with supplier	1	2	3	4	5

18. Which of the following statements best describes the product specifications used by your operation?

    a. Formal, detailed, written specifications
    b. Informal, flexible, unwritten specifications
    c. Formal, flexible, written specifications
    d. Somewhere in between formal and informal
    e. None are used

19. Please select the response that best describes the number of vendors you use annually.

    a. Less than 50
    b. Between 50 and 100
    c. Between 101 and 150
    d. Between 151 and 200
    e. Between 201 and 300
    f. Between 301 and 400
    g. Between 401 and 500

20. During the past 3 years, which best describes the use of new vendors by your firm?

    a. The use has increased significantly
    b. The use has increased moderately
    c. The use has remained constant
    d. The use has decreased moderately
    e. The use has decreased significantly

21. Which best describes the percentage of your vendors which are visited at least annually by a member of your purchasing department?

    a. Less than 10 percent
    b. Between 10 and 25 percent
    c. Between 26 and 50 percent
    d. Between 51 and 75 percent
    e. More than 75 percent

22. In the past 3 years, which best describes the growth of the total number of vendors used by your firm?

    a. The number has increased at a high rate
    b. The number has increased moderately
    c. The number has decreased slightly
    d. The number has decreased significantly

23. During the past 3 years, which best describes the use of international vendors by your company?

    a. The use has increased significantly
    b. The use has increased gradually
    c. The use has decreased gradually
    d. The use has decreased significantly
    e. No offshore vendors are used

THE NEXT TWO QUESTIONS ARE CONCERNED WITH SUPPLIER SELECTION ACTIVITIES...

24. Under which conditions does your firm use a sole source for a particular product or commodity group?

    a. Sole sourcing is used only when no other option is available
    b. Sole sourcing is used only for standard items which can be easily bought elsewhere
    c. Sole sourcing is used for proprietary items
    d. Other (Please specify)_____

25. A list of supplier selection criteria is presented below. Please indicate the importance of these criteria in your operation by circling the correct response. A rating of 1 indicates the criterion is extremely important, while a rating of 5 indicates it is not important.

		Level of Importance			
		Extremely Important		Moderately Important		Not Important
a.	Accuracy in filling orders	1	2	3	4	5
b.	On-time delivery	1	2	3	4	5
c.	Frequency of delivery	1	2	3	4	5
d.	Reasonable lead times	1	2	3	4	5
e.	Willingness to respond in a "pinch"	1	2	3	4	5
f.	Knowledgeable sales staff	1	2	3	4	5
g.	Reasonable payment policy	1	2	3	4	5
h.	Volume discount	1	2	3	4	5
i.	Reasonable minimum order	1	2	3	4	5
j.	Willingness to break a case	1	2	3	4	5
k.	Prompt payment discounts	1	2	3	4	5
l.	Training in product use	1	2	3	4	5
m.	Provision of recipe ideas	1	2	3	4	5
n.	Consistent quality level	1	2	3	4	5
o.	Lowest unit cost	1	2	3	4	5
p.	Reasonable unit cost	1	2	3	4	5
q.	Technical competence	1	2	3	4	5

		Level of Importance				
		Extremely Important		Moderately Important		Not Important
r.	Geographical distance	1	2	3	4	5
s.	Ability to be sole source	1	2	3	4	5
t.	Willingness to work together to resolve problems	1	2	3	4	5

THE ISSUE OF ETHICS IN BUSINESS IS AN ON-GOING CONCERN. LISTED BELOW ARE SEVERAL ACTIVITIES WHICH MAY OCCUR IN NORMAL BUSINESS TRANSACTIONS WHICH MIGHT PRESENT AN ETHICAL DILEMMA. FOR EACH ACTIVITY, PLEASE INDICATE IF YOU BELIEVE THE ACTION IS ETHICAL OR NOT. A RESPONSE OF 1 INDICATES THE PRACTICE IS COMPLETELY UNETHICAL WHILE A RESPONSE OF 5 INDICATES THE PRACTICE IS COMPLETELY ETHICAL. PLEASE CIRCLE YOUR RESPONSE.

26. Gaining information about competitors by asking suppliers for information.

    1) Very unethical   4) Somewhat ethical

    2) Somewhat unethical   5) Ethical

    3) Not sure

27. Allowing physical gifts such as free sales promotion prizes or purchase volume incentive bonuses to be accepted by a purchaser.

    1) Very unethical   4) Somewhat ethical

    2) Somewhat unethical   5) Ethical

    3) Not sure

28. Making statements to an existing supplier that exaggerate the seriousness of a problem in order to obtain better prices or other concessions.

    1) Very unethical   4) Somewhat ethical

    2) Somewhat unethical   5) Ethical

    3) Not sure

29. Giving preferential treatment to suppliers that higher levels of management within your firm prefer or recommend.

    1) Very unethical   4) Somewhat ethical

    2) Somewhat unethical   5) Ethical

    3) Not sure

30. Giving preferential treatment to suppliers that are also good customers.

    1) Very unethical
    2) Somewhat unethical
    3) Not sure
    4) Somewhat ethical
    5) Ethical

31. Allowing free trips, free luncheons or dinners, or other free entertainment to be accepted by a purchaser.

    1) Very unethical
    2) Somewhat unethical
    3) Not sure
    4) Somewhat ethical
    5) Ethical

32. Please identify your company's policy with regard to the acceptance of free trips, luncheons, dinners or other free entertainment.

    a. All gifts must be reported
    b. No reporting required if the value of the gift is less than $25
    c. Reporting required only when the gift exceeds a value of $_____

33. Allowing personalities--liking for one sales representative and disliking for another--to enter into the supplier selection process.

    1) Very unethical
    2) Somewhat unethical
    3) Not sure
    4) Somewhat ethical
    5) Ethical

34. Allowing one or more suppliers to have information on competitors' quotations and allowing such suppliers to requote.

    1) Very unethical
    2) Somewhat unethical
    3) Not sure
    4) Somewhat ethical
    5) Ethical

35. Showing bias against suppliers whose salespeople attempt to reach and influence other departments--such as new product development--directly rather than going through the purchasing department when such avoidance of the purchasing department increases the likelihood of a sale.

    1) Very unethical
    2) Somewhat unethical
    3) Not sure
    4) Somewhat ethical
    5) Ethical

36. Telling an existing supplier the firm is considering using a second source in order to obtain better prices or other concessions.

    1) Very unethical   4) Somewhat ethical
    2) Somewhat unethical   5) Ethical
    3) Not sure

37. Using the firm's economic buying power to obtain better prices or other concessions from suppliers.

    1) Very unethical   4) Somewhat ethical
    2) Somewhat unethical   5) Ethical
    3) Not sure

WHILE THE PREVIOUS SECTION CONSIDERED YOUR RESPONSES TO ETHICAL DILEMMAS, THIS SECTION IS CONCERNED WITH WHICH THE RELATIVE FREQUENCY SUCH ACTIVITIES OCCUR IN THE FOODSERVICE INDUSTRY. FOR EACH ACTIVITY, PLEASE INDICATE IF YOU BELIEVE THE ACTIVITY IS WIDESPREAD OR NOT. A RESPONSE OF 1 INDICATES THE PRACTICE IS WIDESPREAD, WHILE A RESPONSE OF 5 INDICATES THE PRACTICE IS RARELY OBSERVED. PLEASE CIRCLE YOUR RESPONSE.

38. Gaining information about competitors by asking suppliers for information.

    1) Very widespread   4) Somewhat limited occurrences
    2) Somewhat widespread   5) Rarely observed
    3) Average occurrence

39. Allowing physical gifts such as free sales promotion prizes or purchase volume incentive bonuses to be accepted by a purchaser.

    1) Very widespread   4) Somewhat limited occurrences
    2) Somewhat widespread   5) Rarely observed
    3) Average occurrence

40. Making statements to an existing supplier that exaggerate the seriousness of a problem in order to obtain better prices or other concessions.

    1) Very widespread   4) Somewhat limited occurrences
    2) Somewhat widespread   5) Rarely observed
    3) Average occurrence

41. Giving preferential treatment to suppliers that higher levels of management within your firm prefer or recommend.

    1) Very widespread
    2) Somewhat widespread
    3) Average occurrence
    4) Somewhat limited occurrences
    5) Rarely observed

42. Giving preferential treatment to suppliers that are also good customers.

    1) Very widespread
    2) Somewhat widespread
    3) Average occurrence
    4) Somewhat limited occurrences
    5) Rarely observed

43. Allowing free trips, free luncheons or dinners, or other free entertainment to be accepted by a purchaser.

    1) Very widespread
    2) Somewhat widespread
    3) Average occurrence
    4) Somewhat limited occurrences
    5) Rarely observed

44. Allowing personalities--liking for one sales representative and disliking for another--to enter into the supplier selection process.

    1) Very widespread
    2) Somewhat widespread
    3) Average occurrence
    4) Somewhat limited occurrences
    5) Rarely observed

45. Allowing one or more suppliers to have information on competitors' quotations and allowing such suppliers to requote.

    1) Very widespread
    2) Somewhat widespread
    3) Average occurrence
    4) Somewhat limited occurrences
    5) Rarely observed

46. Showing bias against suppliers whose salespeople attempt to reach and influence other departments--such as new product development--directly rather than going through the purchasing department when such avoidance of the purchasing department increases the likelihood of a sale.

    1) Very widespread
    2) Somewhat widespread
    3) Average occurrence
    4) Somewhat limited occurrences
    5) Rarely observed

47. Telling an existing supplier the firm is considering using a second source in order to obtain better prices or other concessions.

    1) Very widespread   4) Somewhat limited occurrences
    2) Somewhat widespread   5) Rarely observed
    3) Average occurrence

48. Using the firm's economic buying power to obtain better prices or other concessions from suppliers.

    1) Very widespread   4) Somewhat limited occurrences
    2) Somewhat widespread   5) Rarely observed
    3) Average occurrence

49. How does your company treat the issue of ethics in purchasing?
    a. Company has a code of ethics which is actively applied
    b. Company has a code of ethics which is used occasionally
    c. Company has a code of ethics but does not monitor it
    d. Company has an unwritten code of ethics

RESPONSES FROM OUR INITIAL STUDY SUGGEST THAT ACCURATE ON-TIME DELIVERY OF ORDERS IS VERY IMPORTANT IN THE CHOICE OF VENDORS. THE FOLLOWING ACTIVITIES REPRESENT METHODS FOR ASSURING SUCH PERFORMANCE. PLEASE INDICATE THE FREQUENCY WITH WHICH SUCH METHODS ARE USED BY YOUR COMPANY. A RESPONSE OF 1 INDICATES THE ACTIVITY IS NORMAL PRACTICE, WHILE A RESPONSE OF 5 INDICATES THE ACTIVITY IS NEVER USED.

50.

	Normal Practice	Frequent Use	Occasional Use	Seldom Used	Never Used
a. Using exclusivity contracts	1	2	3	4	5
b. Paying a somewhat higher per unit price	1	2	3	4	5
c. Providing corporate incentives (for example, offering discounts at your facilities)	1	2	3	4	5
d. Using your purchasing clout	1	2	3	4	5
e. Negotiating long-term contracts with performance clauses	1	2	3	4	5
f. Using multiple sources	1	2	3	4	5
g. Developing a good vendor relationship (for example, prompt payment, reasonable request, shared cost data, etc.)	1	2	3	4	5

THE FOLLOWING QUESTIONS CONCERN THE INDIVIDUAL COMPLETING THE QUESTIONNAIRE. THESE ANSWERS WILL BE HELD IN STRICT CONFIDENCE.

51. Please indicate the number of years you have been in the purchasing profession.

    _____

52. Please indicate the title of your current position. _____

53. Please select the educational level below which represents the highest level of education you have completed.

    a. High school or equivalency
    b. Up to two years of college
    c. Associate degree
    d. Between 2 and 4 years of college
    e. Bachelor's degree
    f. Some graduate level courses
    g. Graduate degree
    h. Other _____

54. Please select the range below which includes your age.

    a. 25 years of age or younger
    b. Between 26 and 32 years of age
    c. Between 33 and 39 years of age
    d. Between 40 and 46 years of age
    e. Between 47 and 53 years of age
    f. Between 54 and 60 years of age
    g. Over 60 years of age

55. Please indicate your gender.

    a. Male   b. Female

56. Please indicate the number of years you have been with this company.

    _____

57. Please indicate the number of years you have been involved in purchasing with this company.

    _____

58. Please indicate in which of the following professional organizations you currently are a member or are interested in becoming a member.

		Currently a Member	Not a Member	Interested in Joining	Not Interested
a.	National Association of Purchasing Management	1	2	3	4
b.	National Restaurant Association	1	2	3	4
c.	American Hotel/Motel Association	1	2	3	4

d. Other: Please List _____

59. Please indicate how frequently you participated in continuing education/professionalization classes in the past year.

   a. No participation
   b. One class
   c. Two classes
   d. Three classes
   e. Four classes
   f. Five classes
   g. More than five classes

60. Please indicate which range below best reflects your annual salary.

   a. Less than $20,000
   b. Between $20,000 and $29,999
   c. Between $30,000 and $39,999
   d. Between $40,000 and $49,999
   e. Between $50,000 and $59,999
   f. Between $60,000 and $69,999
   g. Between $70,000 and $84,999
   h. Greater than $84,999

THANK YOU FOR YOUR TIME AND EFFORTS. YOUR RESPONSES ARE GREATLY APPRECIATED! IF YOU WOULD LIKE A COPY OF THE RESULTS OF THE PRELIMINARY STUDY AND THIS STUDY, PLEASE SEND US A SEPARATE NOTE WITH YOUR NAME AND ADDRESS. THAT WAY, WE CAN ASSURE YOUR CONFIDENTIALITY.

NOTES

CENTER FOR ADVANCED PURCHASING STUDIES •

THE CENTER FOR ADVANCED PURCHASING STUDIES (CAPS) was established in November 1986 as an affiliation agreement between the College of Business at Arizona State University and the National Association of Purchasing Management. It is located at The Arizona State University Research Park, 2055 East Centennial Circle, P.O. Box 22160, Tempe, Arizona 85285-2160 (Telephone [602] 752-2277).

The Center has three major goals to be accomplished through its research program:

- to improve purchasing effectiveness and efficiency
- to improve overall purchasing capability
- to increase the competitiveness of U.S. companies in a global economy

Current research underway includes a Comparative Study of the Purchasing Process in the Manufacturing, Service, Retail/Trade/Distribution, and Government Sectors; Global Purchasing; World-Class Purchasing Organizations and Practices to 1995; Purchasing Roundtable; Purchasing Benchmarking; Impediments to Purchasing from Small Minority-Owned and Women-Owned Suppliers; and Education and Training Requirements and Resources.

CAPS, a 501 (c) (3) not-for-profit research organization, is funded solely by tax-deductible contributions from corporations and individuals who want to make a difference in the state of purchasing and materials management knowledge. Policy guidance is provided by the Board of Trustees consisting of:

R. Jerry Baker, C.P.M., National Association of Purchasing Management
William A. Bales, C.P.M., Union Pacific Railroad
William Bothwell, Northern Telecom Inc.
Montague E. Cooper, C.P.M., Chevron U.S.A., Inc.
Julius J. Edelmann, Del Monte Foods
Harold E. Fearon, C.P.M., Center for Advanced Purchasing Studies and Arizona State University
Michael G. Kolchin, C.P.M., Lehigh University
Robert R. Paul, Lockheed Corporation
Elaine Whittington, C.P.M., Lockheed Aeronautical Systems and the National Association of Purchasing Management

The Center for Advanced Purchasing Studies and the National Association of Purchasing Management wish to thank the following corporations, foundations, individuals, and affiliated purchasing management associations for their financial support:

FIRMS

Americhem Inc.
Ameritech Services
ANR Freight System, Inc.
ARCO
ARGO-TECH Corporation
Avery, Materials Group
Barnes Group Foundation
The Bauer Group
BellSouth Services
BP America
Carter Chemicals & Services, Inc.

Caterpillar Inc.
Chevron, U.S.A., Inc.
C.M. Almy & Sons, Inc.
Coastal Savings Bank
Concord Realstate Corp.
Corning Glass Works
CSX Transportation
Dragon Products Co.
DuPont/Conoco
Eastman Kodak Company
Ernst & Whinney

Exxon Company, U.S.A.
Firestone Trust Fund
Freeway Corp.
G.E. Company, Contracting/Purchasing
G.E. Company, Corporate Sourcing
The Glidden Company
The HCA Foundation
Haluch & Associates
Hughes Aircraft
Imperial Litho/Graphics, Inc.
Intel Corporation

International Minerals & Chemical Corporation
Keithley Instruments, Inc.
Kraft, Inc.
The Lincoln Electric Company
Lockheed Leadership Fund
Loctite Corporation
L-Tec Welding & Cutting Systems
Marathon Oil Company
North Canton Tool Company
Northern Telecom Inc.
NYNEX Materiel Enterprises Co.
Ohio Power Company
Olin Corporation Charitable Trust
OXY USA Inc.
Parker Hannifin Corporation
Polaroid Corporation
Raytheon Company
RJR Nabisco, Inc.
Shamrock Hose & Fitting Company
Shell Oil Company
Simmons Precision Product Inc.
Society Corporation
Southern Pacific Transportation Co.
Texaco Services, Inc.
Texas Instruments Incorporated
TRW Foundation
Union Pacific Railroad Co.
United Technologies Corporation
The Upjohn Company
U S WEST Business Resources, Inc.
Westinghouse Foundation

INDIVIDUALS

Diane K. Bishop
Robert Breitbart
Montague E. Cooper, C.P.M.
Frank Croyl
Walter Eads
Harold E. Fearon, Ph.D., C.P.M.
John H. Hoagland, Ph.D., C.P.M.
Robert L. Janson, C.P.M.
Robert Kaminski, C.P.M.
Dr. Kenneth H. Killen
Frederick W. Ludwig
Paul K. Moffat, C.P.M.
John P. Negrelli
R.D. Nelson
Robert P. Olson, C.P.M.
Harold F. Puff, Ph.D., C.P.M.
Jon E. Schmiedebusch
Stanley N. Sherman, Ph.D., C.P.M.
Jonathan R. Stegner
Arthur W. Todd
Robert F. Weber, Attorney at Law
W. A. Westerbeck
Mr. & Mrs. Harry B. Wiggins

PURCHASING MANAGEMENT ASSOCIATIONS

Akron
Canton
Cinti Demetria
Cleveland
Colorado (Western)
Dayton
Denver
Detroit
District VI
Florida Central
Florida First Coast
Florida Gold Coast
Florida Space Coast
Florida West Coast
Georgia
Iowa (Central)
Iowa (Eastern)
Kansas City
Lima
Madison Area
Maine
Maryland, Inc.
Michigan (Southwestern)
Michigan Assoc. (Western)
New Jersey
New Mexico
New Orleans, Inc.
Oklahoma City
Old Dominion, Inc. (Virginia)
Oregon
Northeastern PA
Petroleum Industry Buyers Group
Philadelphia, Inc.
Pittsburgh
Rhode Island
Spokane
Syracuse and Central New York, Inc.
Tennessee (East)
Toledo
Twin City
Washington (D.C.)
Youngstown District (Ohio)